WRITERS AND THEIR WORK

ISOBEL ARMSTRONG
General Editor

DJUNA BARNES

The Djuna Barnes Archive, University of Maryland

DJUNA BARNES

DJUNA
BARNES

Deborah Parsons

Northcote House
in association with the
British Council

© Copyright 2003 by Deborah Parsons

First published in 2003 by Northcote House Publishers Ltd, Horndon, Tavistock, Devon, PL19 9NQ, United Kingdom.
Tel: +44 (01822) 810066. Fax: +44 (01822) 810034.

British Library Cataloguing-in-Publication Data
A catalogue record for this book is available from the British Library

ISBN 0-7463-1122-2 hb
ISBN 0-7463-0944-9 pb

Typeset by TW Typesetting, Plymouth, Devon
Printed and bound in the United Kingdom by Athenaeum Press Ltd.

Contents

Acknowledgements

I would like to thank Beth Alvarez and her staff at the McKeldin Library, University of Maryland, for their generous help during my research in the Barnes papers, and also the Arts and Humanities Research Board for their grant to facilitate this project. Special thanks also go to my friends and colleagues at the University of Birmingham, particularly Tony Davies, Steve Ellis and Andrzej Gasiorek for their mentorship, and Maria Balshaw, Helena Buffery, Jan Campbell and Liam Kennedy for their generous support and encouragement.

Most importantly, my thanks are due to Isobel Armstrong, for her belief in this project and for her invaluable guidance, to Laura Marcus for her continued inspiration, intellectual encouragement and friendship, and to David Gasca Tucker, for everything.

Biographical Outline

1892	12 June. Born in Cornwall-on-Hudson to Wald and Elizabeth (née Chappell) Barnes.
1910	Common-law marriage with Percy Faulkner.
1912	Attends Pratt Institute, Brooklyn.
1913	Begins work as a journalist for the *Brooklyn Daily Eagle*.
1914	Moves to Greenwich Village; attends the Art Students League of New York.
1915	*A Book of Repulsive Women*, a collection of poems and illustrations, published.
1917	Barnes's paternal grandmother, Zadel, dies.
1921	Paris correspondent for *McCall's* magazine; spends September in Berlin; meets Thelma Wood in Paris.
1923	Living with Thelma at 173, Saint Germain, Paris; *A Book* published.
1927	Barnes and Thelma move to 9, rue Saint-Romain.
1928	*Ryder* published; *Ladies Almanack* privately published in Paris.
1929	Barnes and Thelma separate.
1931	Relationship with Charles Henri Ford; travels with him to Munich, Vienna and Budapest.
1932	Begins writing 'Bow Down' (*Nightwood*); spends Easter in Tangier with Ford; returns to Paris in June for abortion, convalescing at Hayford Hall, England; returns to New York.
1934	Death of Barnes's father and stepmother.
1935	Revising *Nightwood*.
1936	*Nightwood* published by Faber & Faber; returns to Europe in May, living between Paris and London.

1938	Barnes is checked into a nursing home for alcoholism by Peggy Guggenheim.
1939	Returns to New York.
1940	Barnes is committed to a sanatorium on Lake George by brother, Saxon; moves to 5, Patchin Place, Greenwich Village in September.
1945	Barnes's mother dies.
1958	*The Antiphon* published.
1961	*The Antiphon* performed in Sweden.
1968	Double hernia operation.
1970	Thelma Wood dies of cancer of the spine, Connecticut.
1971	Sells papers to the University of Maryland.
1982	18 June. Barnes dies.

Abbreviations

A	*The Antiphon,* from *The Selected Works of Djuna Barnes* (London: Faber & Faber, 1980).
B	*The Book of Repulsive Women: Eight Rhythms and Five Drawings* (Los Angeles: Sun & Moon Press, 1989).
CS	*The Collected Stories of Djuna Barnes,* edited by Phillip Herring (Los Angeles: Sun & Moon Press, 1997).
LA	*Ladies Almanack* (Illinois: Dalkey Archive, 1992).
N	*Nightwood* (London: Faber, 1936)
NY	*New York,* edited by Alyce Barry (Los Angeles: Sun & Moon Press, 1987).
R	*Ryder* (Illinois: Dalkey Archive, 1990).

Introduction

'I hope you will suffer prettily in Paris', Djuna Barnes was politely told by a young child on her arrival in the city from New York in 1922. Recalling the incident Barnes commented, 'I am sure she was much too young to know how astute the words were'.[1] A year later she wrote to her mother: 'Having life is the greatest horror. I cannot think of it as a "merry, gay & joyous thing, just to be alive" – it seems to me monstrous, obscene & still with the most obscene trick at the end'.[2] She was 31 and already a renowned figure amongst the expatriate literary community of the Left Bank. Memoirs of the period describe her beauty, stylish elegance and formidable wit, yet she regarded life as brutal and violating, to be confronted with stubborn fortitude and a satiric tongue. Of her years in Paris she later caustically stated: 'I used to be rather the life of the party. I was rather gay and silly and bright and all that sort of stuff and wasted a lot of time. I used to be invited by people who said "Get Djuna for dinner, she's amusing." So I stopped it'.[3]

Such recollections and anecdotes quickly developed Barnes's cult image of glamorous and intellectual morbidity, yet have also served to long obscure serious recognition of her work that would pay attention to her position within what are increasingly being recognized as the complex and heterogeneous social, historical and aesthetic contexts of modernism. For a brief period Barnes was to become one of the foremost writers of modernist literary Paris, her work described by the critic Edwin Muir as 'the only prose by a living writer which can be compared with that of Joyce'.[4] Despite such acclaim, however, and although her career lasted for over seventy

1

years, Barnes's name has until recently remained marginalized, if not forgotten, by literary academia. This book argues for Barnes's significance within the culture and contexts of Anglo-American modernism, focusing on her four major works, *Ryder*, *Ladies Almanack*, *Nightwood* and *The Antiphon*, as well as her shorter writings and journalism. It aims to introduce the reader to the impassioned despair and unruly hilarity that mark her tone, the visual simplicity and linguistic eccentricity of her expression, and the themes of power, alienation and estrangement that are her focus, but also to highlight her engagement with the social, sexual and aesthetic avant-garde debates of her time.

A bizarre and disturbing childhood, marked by sexual abuse and emotional betrayal, undoubtedly influenced Barnes's bitterly pessimistic view of human nature and existence. She was born on 12 June 1892 in Cornwall-on-Hudson, New Jersey, the daughter of Wald Barnes, a confirmed polygamist, and his English wife, Elizabeth Chappell. Five years later her father began a relationship with another woman, Fanny Faulkner, who over the following ten years would bear him four children in addition to the five he had concurrently with Elizabeth. The Barnes household was thus an eccentric ménage, consisting of both Wald's legitimate and illegitimate families and dominated by the matriarchal presence of his mother. Zadel Barnes had herself been a successful journalist and spirited feminist and reformist campaigner in London in the 1880s, friends with Speranza Wilde and the hostess of a salon for radical thinkers. Burdened with the support of her beloved yet dilettante son, however, she was reduced in old age to making begging visits and writing letters requesting financial aid to friends and relatives in order to keep the family from severe poverty. The emotional repercussions of this strange situation on Djuna, who later revealed that her father had humiliatingly arranged her sexual initiation and also hinted at family incest, remained with her throughout her life. Elizabeth finally separated from Wald in 1912, when he was forced by the law to make a choice between his two 'wives', but Djuna, by this time embarking on her writing career, resented her mother's emotional weakness and financial dependency, and increasingly estranged herself from family ties. She would never forgive either her mother or her grandmother's lack of resistance to her sexual humiliation, which she regarded as acts of ultimate betrayal.

During her childhood Barnes received little formal schooling, the majority of her education undertaken by Zadel. Once in New York, however, she studied art at the Pratt Institute in Brooklyn and at the Art Students League. By 1915 she was writing features for nearly all of New York's newspapers and magazines, and renting her own flat in Greenwich Village, where she moved in the intellectual circle of Village luminaries such as the poet Mina Loy and dramatist Eugene O'Neill. In 1919 Barnes moved to Paris as a correspondent for *McCall's* magazine and soon afterward began a deep yet tempestuous relationship with the American artist Thelma Wood, whom she would describe as her only love and immortalize as Robin Vote in *Nightwood*. During the next fifteen years in Paris Barnes produced her most notable work, *Ryder* and *Ladies Almanack* appearing in 1928 and, after a traumatic break with Thelma, *Nightwood* in 1936, which established her status within the literary avant-garde. She suffered a breakdown in the late 1930s and returned to New York in 1940, publishing her final substantial work, *The Antiphon*, in 1958. Much of the rest of her life was spent as a virtual recluse in Greenwich Village. She died in 1982, six days after her ninetieth birthday.

Djuna Barnes's writing is frequently regarded as difficult and arcane, although many of her articles and short stories are so deceptively simple as to leave the bewildered reader equally perplexed as to their point or meaning. The Dadaist artist Baroness Elsa von Freytag Loringhoven once wrote to her, 'I cannot read your stories Djuna Barnes . . . I don't know where your characters come from', and indeed most are enigmatic and emotionally intense, strangely aware of some alternative sense of being, part sphinx and part sibyl (Barnes's protagonists are typically women or, as in the case of the transvestite doctor, Matthew O'Connor, self-consciously feminine). Some resemble animals or beasts in their instinctive and heavily vacant behaviour; two such are Robin Vote in *Nightwood*, who is described as a 'beast turning human', and the lead character in the short story 'Dusie', who moves 'like vines growing over a ruin'. Others are preternaturally mature children, such as the delicate yet dangerous protagonist of the play *The Dove*, or the young girl who narrates Barnes's Paris stories to her 'Madame'. All seem determinedly self-tormenting to an almost incomprehensible degree. The language characters use, moreover, can also disorientate. Usually parodic and often unrestrained and unsettling, Barnes's writing deals with power, desire and abjection within a culturally exhausted and typically urban milieu, yet she frequently intersperses this with antique diction, robust obscenities and comic satire.

Barnes's focus on perversion and abnormality often led early reviewers to regard her work as imitative of the decadence of the 1890s. By contrast the support and respect she received from Ford Madox Ford, who published her stories in *transatlantic review*, and T. S. Eliot, editor of her tortured masterpiece *Nightwood* (1936), have placed her firmly within the dominant formalist account of literary 'high' modernism. Neither perspective satisfactorily characterizes her work however, and both subordinate the combination of quasi-mystical imagery and rich satire that makes her writing so compelling. Barnes may have moved between the Anglo-American modernist matrix of Greenwich Village, Paris and London, but her aesthetic affinities ranged from Rabelaisian bawdy, to the nineteenth-century fin-de-siècle, to 1930s surrealism. Recent critical interest in Barnes began in the 1970s, with the publication of James B. Scott's *Djuna Barnes* (1976) and Louis F. Kannenstine's *The Art of Djuna Barnes: Duality and Damnation* (1977). A biography by Andrew Field appeared after her death in 1983, offering new material on Barnes's life collected from interviews yet little extended critical discussion of her works. As a result of the achievements of new critical approaches in the 1980s, particularly feminist theory, Barnes has more recently been re-established within scholarly accounts of modernism, and *Nightwood* at least, her best-known and most straightforwardly modernist work, is now part of an accepted, expanded canon. Mary Lynn Broe's *Silence and Power* (1991), a collection of edited essays on different aspects of Barnes's oeuvre, and Phillip Herring's excellent *Djuna* (1995), to which the present reader is directed for full biographical material, are the two works that orchestrated the turning point in Barnes studies and stimulated subsequent scholarly interest. Nevertheless, in general Barnes has remained a problematic and unassimilated presence for both orthodox and revisionary accounts of the literature of the 1920s and 1930s. Peter Nicholls, for example, has described *Nightwood* as a text that stands 'outside' modernism, or at least its dominant formal, transatlantic or gendered conceptualizations.[5]

It would be too simple to situate Barnes's work within either the ubiquitous critical narrative of modernist spiritual and epistemological crisis, or more recent academic interest in the empowering potential of sexual-textual transgression and marginality. There is certainly at times an abstract ahistoricism about her repeated analysis and exposure of Western culture's construction of sexual and more broadly social difference, but the focus of the major novels is ultimately on the grim pain of its effects, as experienced within her own life, within the lives of those around her, and within an increasingly intolerant and politically aggressive Europe. Barnes's fundamental outlook was one of despair at the indifference, even malignancy, of the cosmos, to which the individual, failed by the inadequacy of both religious and psychoanalytical explanations of existence, could only respond with a bitter laugh and grotesque irony. She found fascinating all that seemed to epitomize this perspective, the marginal, grotesque and bizarre figures who offered a mocking reflection of modern identity as social and emotional deformity, and she made it the subject of her best work. On reading the drafts of *Nightwood* in 1935, her friend Emily Coleman wrote to her: 'You make horror beautiful – it is your greatest gift'.[6]

1

Fleur du Mal: Early Writings

'Red cheeks. Auburn hair. Gray eyes, ever sparkling with delight and mischief. Fantastic earrings in her ears, picturesquely dressed, ever ready to live and to be merry: that's the real Djuna as she walks down Fifth Avenue, or sips her black coffee, a cigarette in hand, in the Café Lafayette.'[1]

The confident and lively Djuna Barnes of this description by New York editor and impresario Guido Bruno is a striking image. Framed by Fifth Avenue she becomes a picture of sophisticated urban modernity, by the Café Lafayette, black coffee in hand, an icon of American avant-garde modernism. Bruno was interviewing Barnes in 1919 for *Pearson's Magazine*, as one of the 'Fleurs du mal à la mode de New York', 'Followers of the decadents of France and of England's famous 1890s, in vigorous, ambitious America'. At the dawn of a lucrative career as journalist and interviewer herself, and astutely aware of her smart metropolitan readership, she tells him with studied morbidity, 'We live and suffer and strive, envious and envied. We love, we hate, we work, we admire, we despise . . . Why? And we die, and no one will ever know that we are born . . . Joy? I have had none in my twenty-six years'. In contrast to the raw pain of her Paris reminiscences, Barnes's decadent languidness in this piece is the carefully constructed public pose, of which Bruno, himself an exemplar of bohemian posturing, accuses her. The 'real' Djuna of Bruno's gaze is equally contrived, however, and she ultimately remains elusive and inscrutable.

Barnes's early features and interviews constantly recreate, parody and question accepted images of the city and its inhabitants, acknowledging and revealing them as representational spaces, areas that are experienced through the images and meanings that have come to dominate them. Her articles and stories are often brilliant experiments in genre writing, offering caricatured expressions of the culture and interests of New York society at the beginning of the century. New York in the 1910s was fast becoming the principal city of the early twentieth century, the symbol of all that was new, and the centre of US cultural power and innovation. With its gridded streets and shining towers, it epitomized the ideal of the modern metropolis and was described by the architect and urban planner Le Corbusier as a 'jewel in the crown of cities'. Barnes, however, always drawn as she later admitted to 'jewels with a will to decay', investigated the underside of the city, exploring the liminality of its secular carnivalesque and embarking on a violation of boundaries that would characterize all of her later fiction.

THE BEAUTIFUL AND THE DAMNED

Barnes began her first post as reporter and illustrator for the *Brooklyn Daily Eagle* in the spring of 1913, and by Christmas was invited to the *New York Press* as theatre critic and interviewer by the writer Carl Van Vechten. Over the next few years she became a highly successful and well-paid freelancer, writing regularly for upmarket and high-circulation publications and publishing over one hundred articles and stories. Of the publications to which she contributed regularly, for example, the *Saturday Evening Post* had an average circulation in 1917 of just under 2,000,000, and the smaller and more select, although pervasively influential, *Vogue and Vanity Fair*, about 230,000 between them. *McCall's*, which commissioned Barnes's first articles from Paris, was to become one of the major women's magazines, with an immense readership of 2,000,000 by 1927.[2] These major city newspapers and monthly glossies were marketed to an affluent dilettante and metropolitan readership, one that identified itself through patterns of consumption and demanded constant information on the entertainments, restaurants, fashions and life-styles of the city.

7

Frank Crowninshield, editor of *Vogue* and *Vanity Fair* had set the tone for the new urbane journalism of clever satire and acidic cultural reportage in his editorial for *Vanity Fair*'s opening issue in 1914: 'We as a nation have come to realize the need for more cheerfulness, for hiding a solemn face, for a fair measure of pluck, and for great good humour. *Vanity Fair* means to be as cheerful as anybody. It will print humour, it will look at the stage of the arts, at the world of letters, at sport, and at the highly vitalized, electric and diversified life of our day from the frankly cheerful angle of the optimist, or, which is much the same thing, from the mock-cheerful angle of the satirist'. Barnes was never an optimist but she excelled as a satirist, and the perspective of the 'mock-cheerful' was to become a characteristic of her writing style throughout her life. Adopting the pseudonym of Lydia Steptoe for most of her magazine work from 1922, when she was in Paris and perhaps attempting to distinguish her more serious writing from the magazine work on which she depended for income, she acted the bright New Yorker, conversant in the fashions and preoc-cupations of the young flapper and smart set, but with a sharp eye for the grotesque and the marginal that were their mirror image.

Two articles for *Vanity Fair* illustrate her typically parodic tone and use of decadent rhetoric. 'Against nature', the title the same as the English translation of Joris Karl Huysmans' bible of decadence *À Rebours*, asserts 'Lydia's' credentials as urban sophisticate to her readership: 'I hold advanced ideas but not vulgarly advanced. I just keep prettily ahead of the times, where I show to best advantage, half turned head over shoulder beckoning the generation'.[3] In 'What is Good Form in Dying? In Which a Dozen Dainty Deaths Are Suggested for Daring Damsels', she assumes a chatty familiarity with her readers as, with an earnest eye to fashion, she offers advice on the correct way for women to commit suicide, stating that a stylish death depends on the suitable matching of method with hair colour. The redhead must drown, the blonde 'hang sweetly debonairly, and perseveringly by the neck', and the brunette take a 'slow green poison' in a 'fashionable and well-lit restaurant'.[4] With weary decadent ennui, however, she concludes that for 'the true aristocrat, the real wit, the utterly superior person', the category under which she includes both herself and her reader, the most refined and exquisite death is by boredom. Such pieces exemplify Barnes's journalistic style, written to satisfy, whilst simultaneously mocking, an audience that she considered to be thoroughly manipulable and for whom she had little respect. Her articles may portray the glamorous urban world of Manhattan youth culture and Greenwich Village bohemia, but her knowing use of cliché and insider-gossip on stage-darlings, opening nights, fashion and dance crazes, is imbued with a more critical observation of New York's mass-consumer society.

Not all Barnes's journalism was ironic reportage or coy ephemera, and despite her necessary focus on her bourgeois market, she also used the space of the periodical to voice controversial issues and experimental aesthetics. Although she later dismissed her articles and short stories as ephemeral 'juvenilia', most recent assessments cite them as indicating the origins and development of her distinctive concerns and style, regarding them as precursors of her later, more socio-political and metaphysically orientated fiction.[5] The various interviews, fictions and reports that comprise Barnes's New York writings mingle genres, styles and objectives. Theatre reviews are juxtaposed with documentary reportage, gossip column trivia, stunt reporting, star-interviews, human-interest features, the language of slang and the dance-hall, in an aesthetic mode that draws into a collage the heterogeneous figures and narratives of the modern city.

Her perspective is most commonly that of the urbanite *flâneur*, fascinated by the environment of the metropolis and the popular cultures that reflected the rapidity, fragmentation and exaggeration of experience that it produced, exactly the trivia that Crowninshield recognized as being at the pulse of the modern consumer city, and central to the new urban identities being constructed and promoted by the print media. Traversing 1910s New York, from the Bowery and the Bronx, to the fashions and celebrities of Fifth Avenue and Broadway, and the cultivated bohemianism of Greenwich Village, they convey an imaginative representation of New York's urban geography and socio-cultural scene, as dance-halls, vaudeville theatres, amusement parks, streets of department stores, tramways and elevated railway turned the city into a rich stage of social identities and activities. What draws the journalism, interviews, stories and plays of the early years together is Barnes's keen eye for the theatricality of modernity and the performances of everyday life, an empathy with the outcast, the queer and the unacceptable, and a cynicism towards modern humanity that is coupled with a wry and mocking humour.

The subject matter of Barnes's newspaper articles, for example, draws on a similar vernacular of urban identity to that of the contemporaneous Ashcan artists, presenting literary snapshots of a cross-section of scenes and encounters in the street or entertainment spaces of the city, and highlighting the disjunction between the bourgeois and the popular, the new and the worn, the illusions and the despair to be found across the city landscape. She moves between the elite, the masses and the marginal, from Fifth Avenue and Broadway, streets of fetishistic desire, to Coney Island, spectacle of the ridiculous, and the Lower East Side, repository of the unwanted. Underlying the variously frivolous, investigative or satirical tone that describes these trajectories runs a constant concern with issues of immigration, gender, popular culture and aesthetics within the culture of the city, and an incisive analysis of the construction and performance of cultural identities within the specific map of early twentieth-century New York. In 'The Hem of Manhattan', for example, written in 1917 for the *New York Morning Telegraph*, Barnes takes a pleasure boat around Manhattan Island and contrasts the sights pointed out by the guide (the Brooklyn Bridge and the Flatiron Building) with the more immediate vision of the waterfront, where 'barges heaped with the city's garbage swayed in the greasy, dark water, great mounds of a city's refuse, suspiring in the sun like a glutten lolling after an orgy'.[6]

A feature on Coney Island, also for the *Telegraph*, takes a similarly doubled perspective.[7] Coney had developed as a summer beach resort for the New York elite in the mid-nineteenth century. By the 1900s, however, with the opening by entrepreneur George C. Tilyou of Steeplechase Park, a funfair of technological rides, freakshows and variety performances, followed by Luna Park in 1902 and Dreamland in 1903,

Coney had been transformed into a mecca of mass entertainment. Tilyou's achievement was his provision of attractions for family fun but also thrilling and titillating entertainment that broke down social propriety in a permitted and legitimized irrationality. The most popular rides, for example, were those that encouraged vague promiscuity and sexual indignity; the Human Roulette Wheel, the Barrel of Love, and the Dew-Drop, a circular slide from which a female rider would land on one of sixteen spinning discs, to then be flung around them in wild abandonment. Coney Island stood as an antithesis to the urban sidewalk of the working day, and it became a honeypot for journalists, artists and social theorists eager to observe the hedonistic leisure of modernity. Barnes's article is prefaced by one of her idiosyncratic transgressions, the tale of a mad Russian woman who became disillusioned with the revolution because she regarded modern man as a puppet, too dull for revolt. 'And it was of this woman', states Barnes, 'that I thought as I went through Coney Island' (NY 277).

Recognizing the commercial control of the amusement park, Barnes questions the experience of social release that Coney purported to supply, presenting the visitors to the parks with characteristic satire as passive pleasure-seekers unable to amuse themselves, 'relying instead on the amusement offered them by watching the forced antics of a paid individual who supplied this loss' (NY 277). Bizarre theatricality was always to stimulate Barnes's aesthetic imagination, however, and it is the sideshow performers on whom she concentrates. The sense of the sinister, certainly of the degraded, in the public enjoyment of the grotesque bodies of freaks such as 'THE FATTEST LADY' and 'THE OSSIFIED MAN', prefigures the gender and racial scapegoating of Nightwood, Barnes remarking: 'You look down upon these people as from the top of an abyss, they are the bottom of despair and of life' (NY 279). A young girl who acts as hawker for a photographic booth, 'seems to be an outcome of past cries, curses, shouts, laughter, music, dancing, hubbub, and merry insolence. She is a little girl who has collected herself from the gutter and moulded herself into this saucy, angular body from the refuse of great noises – that are, alas, never grand noises, but the hue and cry of a thousand middlemen making a nickel' (NY 280). This image of the girl as rag-picker, an amalgam of refuse created from the remains of Coney's transient pleasures, offers a personification of the inverse side of modernity's ideology of progress and the new.

Barnes switched easily between the identities of investigative reporter, feature journalist and short story writer. As the various subjects, themes and voices of her articles show, she negotiated her identity as reporter by performing different roles according to the expectations of her different audiences. Thus, for the daily news she offered stunt reporting or scenes of everyday life, for *Vanity Fair* became Lydia Steptoe, and for the Sunday magazines wrote celebrity interviews or melodramatic stories saturated with a strong atmosphere of decadence. Several pieces play on the juxtaposition of roles that Barnes recognizes she is positioned within. 'I was a movie', she states, in an article in which she tries three fire-rescue procedures.[8] Typically, in her job as reporter, Barnes possesses the status of the detached urban observer, a perspective of spectatorial control that critics have identified as a conventionally male privilege. Dangling from a safety rope, however, she is a woman presented as an object for the entertainment of onlookers in the street below, part of a scene made up of 'the rope, the fireman, and the girl'.[9] She becomes the movie itself because, as both observer and observed, camera and celebrity, she embodies the process of filming as well as the object being filmed.

A similar comment on the object status of the female body is made through Barnes's description of 'How It Feels to be Forcibly Fed', for which she underwent the painful and dangerous force-feeding that was administered to British suffragettes on hunger strikes.[10] The article is accompanied by an elegant portrait photograph of 'Miss Djuna Chappell Barnes', and a series of photographs in which Barnes lies on an operating table, covered in a white sheet and surrounded by physicians as they insert the feeding tube into her nose. In these pictures she has become merely a physical object, whose autonomy is denied by the doctors as they force food into her body. Half fainting, she is unable to focus on the doctors or the room around her, and is aware only of the pain in her head and the sensation of cold liquid falling in her throat. 'I had lapsed into a physical mechanism', she states, 'without power to oppose or resent the outrage to my will'.[11] The article is again ambiguous in its stance however, undoubtedly expressing sympathy for Barnes's 'English sisters' who had experienced such suffering, yet ultimately refusing support or censure of either agitists or physicians. The photographs of Barnes reduce her to an object of medical observation, but in the article itself, despite the horrors of her pain, she retains the identity of investigative reporter, curiously undergoing treatment as a voluntary 'experiment'. With little belief in collective political polemic, Barnes obstinately resisted social and political categorization throughout her life and writing. The apolitical, documentary tone of the article may have been intended to suit the sensibilities of her bourgeois audience, but it also suggests Barnes's own ambivalence towards a suffragist narrative of self-sacrifice, martyrdom and bodily denial promoted by hunger striking.

Barnes's attempt to balance her identities as journalist and burgeoning modernist are also evident in a number of articles, part gossip, part guidebook and part satire, that she wrote on Greenwich Village, the bohemian enclave neighbouring the commercial heart of the city. Once an affluent residential area, as the urban elite moved uptown its picturesque townhouses had been subdivided into lodgings, and the cheap rents encouraged an ethnically and culturally diverse population of artists, writers and, to the south and south-east, Irish, Italian, Jewish and Chinese immigrants. Such multiculturalism suited the artists rebelling against a censorious Protestant heritage and the dull commercialism of contemporary capitalism, although any identification was largely exoticized and superficial. Not only was the secular liberalism of the artist community anathema to the immigrant cultures, but its nonconformity was also perceived by wider society with indulgence, and made the object of fashionable interest rather than social criticism. During the 1910s the Village was the hub of New York aesthetic, political and moral experimentalism, presided over by Mabel Dodge, the self-styled patroness of modern art, who gathered leading avant-garde writers, artists, editors and critics, as well as political radicals and other social nonconformists, to 'Evenings' at her apartment at 23 Fifth Avenue. Barnes herself not only lived in the Village but her friends

13

included the leading names of New York modernism; the writers Mina Loy, William Carlos Williams and Marsden Hartley, the painter Marcel Duchamp and playwright Eugene O'Neill, photographers Alfred Stieglitz and Berenice Abbott, critics Malcolm Cowley and Kenneth Burke, Charlie Chaplin, and the editors of the *Little Review*, Jane Heap and Margaret Anderson. Introduced to Dodge by Carl Van Vechten, she would later partly model Nora Flood and her bizarre bohemian salon in *Nightwood* on her.

In her three features on the Village written in 1916, the first for *Pearson's Magazine*, and two for the more populist *New York Morning Telegraph Sunday Magazine*, Barnes offers different narratives of the area and its inhabitants, balancing her insider knowledge with an astute awareness of the demands of her various readerships. In 'Greenwich Village as it is', for example, for *Pearson's*, she states that her aim is 'to dispel some of the false notions' about the Village, and she appeals to the reader to look beyond its marketed image as a bohemia of poets and intellectuals following decadent lives and conducting scandalous sexual relations. With the authority of being herself a Villager she thus conversely notes the figures that are ignored by the eye of fashion: 'We have our artists but we also have our vendors. We have our poets, but we also have our undertakers. We have our idlers, but have we not also our scrubwomen?' Indeed her tone is if anything defiant as she rejects the realist reportage that the title of the piece seems to demand: 'To have to tell the truth about a place immediately puts that place on its defence. Localities and atmospheres should be let alone'.[12] In the sketches for the *Morning Telegraph*, however, Barnes exaggerates the stereotype of Greenwich Village to satisfy the expectations of her bourgeois readership. 'Becoming Intimate with the Bohemians' opens with the waking of the King and Queen of Bohemia late in the afternoon, as the cafés and bars begin to fill with recognizable stock types: girls in smocks of exotic fabrics, a handsome foreigner who is perhaps Italian, perhaps Russian, a frail-looking artist, a girl with a 'past'. Observing the scene, Barnes is approached by a woman in fur and jewels, bourgeois 'Madam Bronx', who comes to the Village as a tourist, searching the area for a souvenir glimpse of the bohemian and chasing off after Floyd Dell, Max Eastman and Marsden Hartley. She would probably have been amply satisfied by a glimpse of the studio flat that Barnes describes:

> Blue and yellow candles pouring their hot wax over things in ivory and things in jade. Incense curling up from a jar; Japanese prints on the wall. A touch of purple here, a gold screen there, a black carpet, a curtain of silver, a tapestry thrown carelessly down, a copy of Rogue on a low table open at Mina Loy's poem. A flower in a vase, with three paint brushes; an edition of Oscar Wilde, soiled by socialistic thumbs.[13]

The scene seems carefully contrived, a picture for the interiors pages of a fashion magazine. The satire continues in the second article, 'How the Villagers Amuse Themselves', in which Barnes parodies both the fashionable fascination with pseudo-bohemian culture and the frivolous identification of Villagers themselves with their 'decadent' image. 'It's a hard life', she mockingly sighs, 'for down here one has not only to live up to one's blue china – an occupation much lamented by Wilde – but they have also to live up to their jade and antiquities, not to mention their sullied reputations'.[14]

THE BOOK OF REPULSIVE WOMEN

Guido Bruno was just one figure to shrewdly recognize the financial benefit of promoting the risqué image of Greenwich Village to the bourgeois tourist, consolidating and overtly advertizing the notion of decadent Village bohemianism in his cultural magazine *Bruno's Weekly*. Barnes, a member of the Provincetown Players, journalist, poet and illustrator, was an ideal figure for such commercial promotion. *The Book of Repulsive Women*, eight decadent-style poems, accompanied by five Beardsleyesque drawings, was published by Bruno in 1915 and exemplified the image he wanted to promote of the Baudelairean morbidity of the cultural enclave of the Village. Although contemporary with Barnes's socialite columns and features, the poems collected in *The Book of Repulsive Women* offer a series of portraits of women in states of physical and moral degeneration, and counter the slender and civilized images found within the pages of the glossies with overt and

15

grotesque depictions of the fluids and emissions of the female body. Being written for Bruno they were probably intended for an outside market, but to dismiss them, as does Phillip Herring, as 'disgusting', is to ignore Barnes's expertise in writing at once for and against the values of her audience.[15]

Barnes certainly both lucratively performed and playfully mocked the bohemian stereotype, but she also used explicit decadent images in her early work for specific purpose – as a language with which to voice the unacceptable margins of the secular carnivalesque. Juxtaposing images of monstrous ageing with acts of diseased lesbianism, the poems expose the double standards of modern gender relations and a capricious cult of youth that lead only to self-mockery and ultimately self-disgust. Taken from different perspectives in the city land-scape, the heights of Fifth Avenue, the tenements below Third Avenue, the EL, the gutter and the cabaret saloon, the poet-narrator constructs these women as spectacles of a male-oriented viewpoint. Barnes continues her journalistic focus on consumer society's permissive morality, commodification of youth, and ethos of individual success and compulsive amuse-ment, but twists perspective to explore the sordid and forbid-den spaces of a body/street map of the city. In contrast to the phallic power or slender female muse associated with the vertical lines of the skyscraper, she draws a parallel between the fleshly female body of unleashed female physicality and the unknowable, disordered space of lower Manhattan, both of which rebel against the ideal constructions of consumer fashion, emitting unspeakable fluids and wastes.

The poems represent the ambivalence of masculine construc-tions of desire, in which woman is fantasized as either, or both, angel and whore, sacred and profane, beauty and beast. Rather than feminist icons of rebellion however, the women of the poems are typically victims of a society in which the demands of continual youth, beauty and purity are prevalent and yet in tension with a coexistent social ideology of emancipation, as experienced for example by the vacant-eyed young woman of 'From Third Avenue', who has undergone an abortion with 'A little conscience, no distress'. In another poem, 'Seen From the "L"', the poet observes a nude woman dully combing her hair in a dusty room. The elevated train presented a new level of urban visuality, between that of the street and the skyscraper, and a vantage point on previously invisible city spaces, for example the upper-level rooms of New York's shabbier districts. Although the woman's window faces 'starkly toward the street', she does not attempt to conceal herself from the view from the 'L'; 'She does not see, she does not care/It's always there'. The sighting from the passing elevated train however can only be brief, and the remainder of the poem constructs an imaginary character for the opaque image glimpsed in an ephemeral moment. That the woman is single and lives in meagre dwellings could suggest struggling independence, but her lack of modesty at the window is taken by the prying gaze of the passing traveller to imply immorality, that she is 'Slipping through the stitch of virtue,/ into crime'. In the vague image from the moving train, the only feature to stand out is the paint of her lips, 'vivid and repulsive'.

Barnes was recognizing that, in New York, emancipation operated within limits, contained by the invisible social gridlines of the newly crystalline city's well-planned map. 'To a Cabaret Dancer' portrays the corrupting influence of the commercially sexualized urban space and body. In the persona of a member of the cabaret audience, Barnes relates the tale of a young dancer, laughing and graceful, who 'looked between the lights and wine/ For one fine face' (B 31). Her idealism soon abates however, and finding

> life only passion wide
> Twixt mouth and wine
> She ceased to search, and growing wise
> Became less fine

> (B 31–2)

Fast living gradually destroys her beauty, the colour leaves her cheeks, her eyes become bloodshot and her lips turn 'a ruined crimson'. What is particularly notable about the poem is the responsibility that the narrator accepts for the dancer's demise. For the audience's enjoyment seems to emanate from ridiculing her as a freak show. It is 'the jests that lit our hours by night/ And made them gay' that soil her, and the forty sneers and thousand jibes that drive her to dejection, though she continues to perform and the audience continues to jeer. For both dancer and audience seem caught in a dialectic of attraction and revulsion, in which

> Until her songless soul admits
> Time comes to kill:
> You pay her price and wonder why
> You need her still.

(B)

The inevitable future of the urban woman, for whom the practice of sexual emancipation is only briefly sanctioned, would seem to be fragmentation, dissolution and self-destruction.

In the final poem, 'Suicide', two female corpses offer themselves as nothing more than objects for the observer's gaze. The first covered in bruises that form 'shattered symphonies', the second, 'her body shock-abbreviated/ As a city cat', they are simply broken commodities, refuse from the street. If Broadway was the artery of New York's glamorous star culture, a glittering but fragile world, then the Bowery was the city's kidney, the gathering space for the unwanted and abject. It is exactly the past, the derelict and the unwanted, however, and their persistence within the netherworld of the city, that fascinated Barnes and pervades her articulation of the New York landscape, a challenge to a modernist canon of vigorous metropolitanism that celebrated the city's skyscraper linearity. It would be a similar sense of the urban abject, and its surreal ability to retain the unconscious, passional or irrational forces of a palimpsestic past, that would form the nocturnal landscape of Paris in *Nightwood*.

TOWARDS MODERNISM

After *The Book of Repulsive Women*, Barnes worked increasingly on short stories and highly stylized one-act dramas. The latter were written more for the page than the stage, focusing on witty dialogue or dramatic monologue rather than plot or action, although *Three From the Earth*, *Kurzy of the Sea*, and *An Irish Triangle* were produced by the Provincetown Players in their 1919–20 season, and another, *The Dove*, by Studio Theatre

18

in 1926. It was with the regular publication of stories in the *Little Review*, however, after Margaret Anderson and Jane Heap moved the magazine from Chicago to New York in 1918, that Barnes began to establish a reputation as a leading modernist writer. Between 1914 and 1929 the *Little Review* provided the principal forum for modernist avant-garde creativity, publishing Ezra Pound, T. S. Eliot, Wyndham Lewis, Gertrude Stein, H.D., Marianne Moore, Dorothy Richardson, May Sinclair and, perhaps most famously, James Joyce's *Ulysses*, as well as printing reproductions of work by Jean Cocteau, Juan Gris and Joseph Stella. Barnes published seven stories in the *Little Review* between 1918 and 1921 when she went to Paris, all but the first of which were reprinted in the collection of stories, plays and drawings, *A Book*, published by Boni & Liveright in 1923. They continue the aura of decadence typical of her writing at this time, combined with a bizarre set of characters who suffer extreme but often inexplicable emotional torment. Most of the stories published in *A Book*, and in Barnes's later collections, have rather nebulously identified but seemingly European settings and protagonists. Dealing predominantly with encounters of human agony and human indifference, the various protagonists carry a weight of subjective tension, the psychological motivations for which remain impenetrable.

American reviews struggled with the subjective focus and European influence of *A Book*, the *New York Times* describing the collection as 'casual episodes of our American life against the background of a Continental structure', 'American in tradition and feeling, but with sufficient acquaintance with European standards and particularly with European literary expression', and 'the American mind and behaviour in its most individual aspiration and in the style of a French analyst', whilst admitting that 'there is no American character'. The reviewer lavishes praise, stating that 'the purpose is clear and logical, and the style graphic, keen and discerning. This discernment is not unworthy of a Balzac and the artistry not unbecoming to a de Maupassant', but seems thrown by the panoply of non-American protagonists and eventually decides that Barnes presents a 'universality of human thought and endeavour', as would T. S. Eliot in his preface to *Nightwood*. Paradoxically, however, his summary implies exactly the differentiation of American and European identity that he attempts to deny and that Barnes was developing in these early stories. 'I think a child is born corrupt and attains to decency' states one character in 'Oscar', and 'Religion is a design for pain' says another in 'The Robin's House'. For Barnes, human identity might have universal origin, but this early, even pre-infant state is irrevocably suppressed by social and particularly by religious conditioning, and in *Nightwood* she would portray the American mind as tragically repressed by a Protestant heritage of self-denial. Robin Vote is the exception, a strangely naïve yet age-old figure who is unconscious of established morality, and prototypes for her character are evident in the child murderer Oscar, and the eerie young girl known as the Dove.

The Dove, a one-act play later performed by Studio Theatre in 1926, presents a claustrophobic atmosphere of sexual repression and tension, and suggests the influence of Ibsen, Chekhov or Shaw in its subordination of action to psychology and symbolism. The play's protagonists are two sisters, Amelia and Vera Burgson, and a young girl they have befriended and invited to live with them, whom Amelia has nicknamed 'the Dove'. The setting is the Burgson's apartment, which the stage directions describe as follows: 'decoration is garish, dealing heavily in reds and pinks. There is an evident attempt to make the place look luxuriously sensual'. Swords, firearms and pistols are everywhere, on the walls or lying on chairs. The act opens with Vera lying on a sofa, as the Dove sits polishing a sword. Much of the dialogue between them plays with sexual innuendo and allusion to the sinister, but Vera's hints of her and Amelia's depravity, their knowledge of French jokes and indecent 'yellow' books, create only a parody of decadent sensuality. The atmosphere of perversity is carefully contrived, a desperate attempt to play out repressed fantasies of sexuality and violence in a pathetic sham of corrupt eroticism. Vera's cry that 'we'll never, never be perverse' is a declaration of enforced virginity that reveals sexual frustration. The Dove, on the other hand, who at first seems a figure of innocence, increasingly appears more sinister, calmly cleaning the sword as she refers to her 'unnatural past' and hints at incest with her brothers and father. Vera tells her that she is afraid of her, and that 'It's just like Amelia to call the only dangerous thing she ever knew the "Dove" '.

Amelia then returns, having gone out to buy butter, and calls attention to a painting hanging in their hallway, off-stage, of *Deux courtisanes vénitiennes* by the late-Renaissance painter Carpaccio, a particularly popular print in Victorian England. It offers a visual extension to the play's theme of sexual tension, depicting two languid women on a balcony, one of them looking up from playing with two dogs, both in stark profile and staring at something beyond the left frame of the picture. In one corner is a small boy, in front of the women a peacock, a parrot and a pair of red shoes, and on the balustrade two doves, symbols of love, and a pomegranate, symbol of fertility. Amelia has bought a bottle of wine, which Vera goes to uncork, and once alone with the Dove walks agitatedly around the room, seemingly made claustrophobic by its walls and complaining of her lack of a lover: 'Why should I wear red heels? Why does my heart beat?' Her talk becomes increasingly hysterical and she tries to grab the sword from the Dove, clutching her hand instead, at which the Dove bites into her shoulder and breast. As Vera reappears the Dove takes up a pistol and walks off-stage, where she shouts, 'For the house of Burgson!' as a shot is fired. Amelia runs after her and returns with the painting, a bullet hole through its centre, crying, '*This is obscene*'.

Studio Theatre's production of *The Dove* was received with bewilderment by theatre critics. A perplexed reviewer for the *New York Sunday Telegraph* declared, 'It is, one fancies, a study of inhibitions in the fin-de-siècle period and shows, perhaps, what awful things inhibitions were in those days. It gives an effect rather such as one might expect to obtain if, say, one were to read Stein on a merry-go-round, by candlelight. But so lamentably few of us have had such experiences', commenting sardonically on the title that 'it had to be called something and doves had as much connection with it as anything else. Save, perhaps, bats'.[16] *The Evening Post* described it as 'pseudo-Freud, Neo-Shaw, Pre-Barrie . . . a wearisome talk orgy wherein the action is supposed to be reduced to the fine points of Freudian symbolism'.[17] What such critiques miss, however, is the parodic and critical element of Barnes's presentation, in which it is exactly the limitations of reductionist Freudian symbolism, and the pseudo-profundity that they accuse her of stumbling into, that are being mocked. The explosion of interest in Freudian psychoanalytic theory in the 1910s and 1920s, provided an important context for the social and aesthetic milieu of Greenwich Village. The writings of Havelock Ellis, advocating a broader range of sexual impulses, introducing the notion of the congenital invert, and legitimating new, less socially restrictive sexual experiences, had quickly gained vogue in the United States and particularly taken root in the self-conscious bohemianism of Greenwich Village. Freudianism was influential by the mid 1910s, popularized by American psychoanalysts as a form of confession of sexual desire and a celebration of the libido as a creative energy force.

Psychoanalysis thus made available new awareness of psychic identity, encouraging the recognition and exploration of alternative narratives of the self in relation to its temporal, social and spatial environment. Yet at the same time it claimed authoritative explanatory knowledge of the psychological causes of external symptoms, knowledge that could be exaggerated into a formulaic method of question, answer and interpretation. Barnes's plays and stories from her Greenwich Village years mock the fashion for psychoanalysis in the popular imagination, teasing her audience and readers with overt symbolic elements that nevertheless refute attempts at interpretation. The reader frantically examines the text for meaning but is often left in bewilderment, defeated by its opacity, or, like one critic, complaining that Barnes's work is ultimately merely a 'locked box with nothing in it'. Lawrence Langner, one of the few early scholars to comment on Barnes's plays, writes that she 'combined a startling sense of dramatic values with an incoherence of expression that made everything she wrote exciting and baffling at the same time'.[18] The question that perplexed the theatre audience of *The Dove*, for example, was quite *what* was obscene; the lifestyle of the two sisters, the picture, the Dove's hints of incest and lesbianism, the shooting, the play itself?

The problem is not just that Barnes confounds traditional narrative convention – in modernism this is to be expected and desired – but that she also seems to refuse the subtext upon which the reader has instead become reliant. Barnes's works are not particularly about character. Her protagonists resemble silhouettes, or marionettes, who present angular and impenetrable exteriors. Often bizarre and emotionally or physically abusive, and frequently involved in mysterious relationships of strange intensity, they seem to respond to forces which remain inaccessible to the reader. This continues into her later writing, where again she does not typically foreground consciousness or a subconscious, if anything hinting at a blood-consciousness that seems to align more with theories of degeneration and primitivism than with psychoanalysis.

THE PARIS STORIES

By the 1920s Barnes's desire to write serious modern fiction was increasingly clashing with her financial need to write journalism. Moreover, with the expatriation of Gertrude Stein and Ezra Pound to Paris, Greenwich Village seemed to have become culturally moribund and little more than a commercialized tourist attraction, the centre of modernist production shifting to Europe. In 1921 Barnes was sent to Paris on an assignment for the magazine *McCall's*, where she would remain intermittently during the 1920s and 1930s, until her breakdown in 1939 enforced return to New York. Alongside her journalism she was by now also writing fiction and drama for the small, private publications committed to promoting and establishing experimental literature, including the *Little Review* and the *Dial*, and in Paris the *transatlantic review* and *transition*. It was not until the 1930s, however, after the success of her novel *Ryder*, that she would feel adequately financially secure to prioritize her literary work over her journalism.

It was in Paris that Barnes wrote what are probably her best stories; 'Aller et Retour', published by Ford Madox Ford in *transatlantic review* in 1924, and a group of four tales of erotic encounters narrated by a young girl to an enigmatic Madame, 'Cassation', 'The Grande Malade', 'Dusie' and 'Behind the Heart'.[19] 'Aller et Retour' is the story of Madame von Bartmann, a Russian living in Paris, whose estranged husband has recently died and who travels to Nice to visit the daughter that she has not seen in seven years. Exuding an air of sophisticated ennui, she is another of Barnes's gallery of decadent characters, in contrast to the rural innocence of her daughter Richter. Cold and aloof, she counsels Richter from the world-weary and bitter perspective of the knowing cosmopolitan: ' "Life," she said, "is filthy; it is also frightful. There is everything in it: murder, pain, beauty, disease – death. Do you know this?" [. . .] "Think everything, good, bad, indifferent; everything, and *do* everything, *everything*! Try to know what you are before you die" ' (*CS* 369, 371). When Richter presents her fiancé, a young clerk, she is at once surprised and relieved. Her final words, 'Ah, how unnecessary' (*CS* 373), spoken in the train back to Paris, might refer both to the pointlessness of her journey and to her daughter's conventional decision to marry.

The narrator of the 'Little Girl' stories is a much younger cosmopolitan woman Katya, who seems to travel freely and independently around Europe's cities. According to Charles Henri Ford, she was based on Tylia Perlmutter, one of two Dutch sisters who sat as models for the Parisian avant-garde and who Barnes also wrote of in her article for *Charm* in 1924, 'The Models Have Come to Town'.[20] In Barnes's stories Tylia becomes both writer and muse, narrating stories in whose eroticism she is also implicated. The tone and style of her speech make her seem younger than her nineteen years, assuming the voice of the innocent naïf. The 'Madame' whom she addresses is older and remains silent, but the atmosphere between them, as of the stories themselves, is one of mute eroticism, the original titles of the early stories – 'A Little Girl Tells a Story to a Lady' and 'The Little Girl Continues', both published in 1925 and later revised and retitled as 'Cassation' and 'The Grande Malade' for the *Spillway* collection – accentuating the vaguely incestuous nature of their relationship.

The first tale is set in Berlin, which Barnes had visited for some months in 1921. 'Do you know Germany, Madame, Germany in the spring?' (*CS* 382), Katya begins, going on to recall how she used to regularly see a tall and wealthy-looking woman as she sat in a café at one end of the Zelten garden. After some time they speak and the woman, Gaya, invites her to stay in her house. Katya tells Madame that 'I said I would meet her again some day in the garden, and we could go "home" together, and she seemed pleased, but did not show surprise' (CS 384). Her forwardness hints at a context for her nomadic lifestyle, implying that her vocation is partly that of a female gigolo, although she states that she aims to be a dancer in the ballet. One evening they sit together in the garden, listening to the orchestra, and, when they leave, it is separately and in silence, Katya following the older woman, who leaves 'a small rain of coin' (CS 384) as she exits, whether for the performers or for Katya is not revealed. Gaya takes her straight to a large bedroom, 'disorderly, and expensive and melancholy' (CS 384), dominated by a large bed with a huge war painting above it, in which 'generals, with foreign helmets and dripping swords, raging through rolling smoke and the bleeding ranks of the dying, seemed to be charging the bed, so large, so rumpled, so devastated' (CS 385). It is a space of birth and of torture, at once the womb and inferno. In the midst of the bed Katya finally spies a child, Gaya's mentally backward daughter Valentine, 'making a thin noise, like the buzzing of a fly' (CS 385).

In a fairytale plot, Gaya puts Katya in another bedroom above her own chamber, even more womb-like, with curtains, bedspread and cushions in deep red velvet, where she stays for a year, living in a strange, hypnotic passivity. It is not until Gaya finally asks her to stay permanently to look after the child that she decides she must leave, frightened by the fanaticism of the woman's commands. Carolyn Allen argues that Gaya intends Katya to look after the child, as she is helpless to attend to its needs herself, yet her desire for Katya also suggests that she sees her as its replacement.[21] Demanding 'You must forget all the things people have told you. You must forget argument and philosophy', she wants Katya to decline to the mindless, animal state of her child, pathetically promising that 'You will like it, you will learn to like it the very best of all. [. . .] I will hold you on my lap, I will feed you like the birds. I will rock you to sleep' (CS 389). Katya leaves but makes a final visit before departing Berlin, to find Gaya in bed with the child, making its same buzzing sound.

'The Little Girl Continues', set in Paris, directs the reader to the sequential connection of the two stories and introduces

Katya's younger sister Moydia. The sisters' cosmopolitanism is emphasized – 'We are where we are. We are Polish when we are in Poland, and when in Holland we are Dutch, and now in France we are French, and one day we will go to America and be American' (CS 394) – but also the distinction between the boyish Katya and the lively and feminine Moydia. Moydia, who cultivates an image of theatrical bohemianism, becomes involved in a triangulate relationship with two men, a Baron and his protégé, Monsieur X, who becomes her lover. While she is out of town, visiting her father, Monsieur X dies and the Baron gives the dead man's cape to Katya as a memento for Moydia. Moydia returns and spends a night crying, but by the next day has forgotten her grief and is quite well. The story is of an almost momentary passion in the girls' nomadic life, the fickleness of the coquette and the cruel indifference of human beings. Two years later Moydia is 'gay, spoiled, *tragique*' (CS 403), and Katya closes the story, 'now we must be moving on' (CS 403).

If sexual tension and homosexuality is implicit in the first two stories, 'Dusie', written in 1927 towards the end of Barnes's relationship with Thelma Wood, takes an overtly lesbian subject: the relationship of Madame K and her child-like lover Dusie, who, 'tall, very big and beautiful, absent and pale' (CS 404), directly prefigures the character of Robin Vote in *Nightwood*. Her 'strong bodily odour' (CS 407), 'ferocious and oblivious vulgarity' (CS 406), and her movements, which resemble 'vines growing over a ruin' (CS 407), anticipate, for example, the description of the somnambulant Robin when she is first discovered by the Doctor and Baron Felix in her bedroom in the Hôtel Récamier. Again prefiguring *Nightwood*, and the relationship of Robin and Nora Flood, the wealthy and childless Madame K, who runs a women-only salon, adopts an erotic but also maternal role, to which Dusie clings. While Madame K is away, Dusie invites Katya back to their house, where they lie in bed until another woman, Clarissa, who also has a key to the house, arrives. Katya moves into another room and when she wakes the following morning finds Dusie crying in bed, her foot 'all crushed, and lying helpless' (CS 411), just before Madame K returns. The events of the night remain a mystery, but the senseless violence is again that of *Nightwood*,

26

implying the painful passion and destructiveness of lesbian love.

The final story to 'Madame' was written some years later and is perhaps one of the most sensitive that Barnes ever wrote, an autobiographical account of her affair with the young writer Charles Henri Ford, detailing her illness and their subsequent friendship. It is far more romantic in tone than the earlier tales, presenting the love of a woman and a 'little boy' (Barnes was 39, Ford 21), their sexual relationship and his eventual evasion of commitment, although in fact he asked her to marry him at least twice.[22] It is mainly a celebration of Ford himself, his youth and physical beauty. That 'Behind the Heart' was never published in her lifetime is perhaps testimony to Barnes's sensitivity over its personal content, for although she quickly scorned Ford after the relationship finished, calling him 'Charles "Impossible" Ford', the story suggests that her feeling for him was greater than she admitted, and that his capricious nature hurt her deeply: 'And she was trembling in the dark, and she went away into the bedroom, and stood with her back to the wall, a crying tall figure in the dark' (CS 454).

27

2

A Female Comic Epic: *Ryder*

'I am writing the female Tom Jones'[1]

One of Barnes's early assignments in Paris was her interview with James Joyce for *Vanity Fair* in 1922, in which she described *Ulysses* as 'that great Rabelaisian flower'.[2] Her first novel, *Ryder* (1928), offered her own tribute to Rabelais, a modern parody by a *female* writer of the bawdy and satiric style of the eighteenth-century comic epic. It rather surprisingly became a brief bestseller on its publication in New York, securing Barnes's reputation within the expatriate modernist circle and relieving her financial dependency on magazine work. Some degree of *Ryder*'s initial success might be put down to public curiosity, aroused by its censorship and consequent reputation as dangerously risqué. *Ryder* was just one of a number of works that famously fell foul of literary censorship in the 1920s, including Joyce's *Ulysses*, Radclyffe Hall's *The Well of Loneliness* and D. H. Lawrence's *Lady Chatterley's Lover*. When the novel was seized by the New York Post Office, Barnes was forced to remove passages referring to bodily fluids or religious blasphemy, along with several of her illustrations.[3] The final published version included a defiant foreword written by Barnes from Paris:

> This book, owing to censorship, which has a vogue in America as indiscriminate as all such enforcements of law must be, has been expurgated. Where such measures have been thought necessary, asterisks have been employed, thus making it matter for no speculation where sense, continuity, and beauty have been damaged.
> That the public may, in our time, see at least a part of the face of creation (which it is not allowed to view as a whole) it has been thought the better part of valour, by both author and publisher, to

make this departure, showing plainly where the war, so blindly waged on the written word, has left its mark.

Hithertofore the public has been offered literature only after it was no longer literature. Or so murdered and so discreetly bound in linens that those regarding it have seldom, if ever, been aware, or discovered, that that which they took for an original was indeed a reconstruction.

In the case of Ryder they are permitted to see the havoc of this nicety, and what its effects are on the work of the imagination. (*R* vii)

What remained, however, was far from prudish, and instead remained so shockingly frank that one reviewer in the *New York Evening Sun*, referring to the expurgations, commented that, 'In spite of this cautiousness, I doubt that the book is sold openly in Boston'.[4] Described by the *Evening Post* as, 'the very backlash of Puritanism', it upturned literary, religious and sexual orthodoxy through linguistic and thematic misrule.

THE FAMILY TREE

Ryder is at once a picaresque novel, social satire and eccentric family chronicle, but also a parable of the politics of sexual reproduction. Barnes's style, however, in the words of one recent reviewer, 'honors no boundaries and makes no concessions'.[5] In *Ryder* she eschews the conventional chronology and realist style of the family saga, which is told as if from hindsight, thus merging past, present and future. The stylized language and diction mimic earlier literary periods, notably that of Chaucerian verse and the Restoration drama which expressed the tone of a post-Puritan age through bawdy frivolity and unrestrained blasphemy. The subtle juxtaposition and reworking of styles and genres, however, along with breaks in the conventional linearity of plot and narrative, indicate the strategies of modernism. The plot, as much as there is one, is based closely on Barnes's childhood on Storm Mountain and tells the story of Wendell Ryder, an instinctive polygamist who lives on a homestead with his mother, his wife and his mistress, along with their eight children.

The early chapters of the book present a brief history of the family, introducing Sophia Ryder, her son Wendell and his future wife Amelia, their life in England and relocation to America, and the arrival of Kate Careless, a friend of Sophia's from London who becomes Wendell's mistress. The focus then turns to accounts of Wendell's repeated infidelities, his ever-growing family, and the peculiar domestic events of the Ryder household. Refusing to conform to the dictates of puritan mores, Wendell houses his two families, one by Amelia and one by Kate, in attempted harmony under one roof, rejecting the rigidity of the local school, and insisting on the children being educated at home. After increasingly threatening demands by Church and school that Wendell submit to their social law, he is accused of immorality and told to sacrifice his lifestyle or face prosecution.

Ryder is Barnes's most overtly autobiographical work, and both Andrew Field and Phillip Herring in their biographies emphasize the context of Barnes's childhood on the Long Island farm and the direct parallels between Wendell and Sophia Ryder and Barnes's father and grandmother. Wald Barnes's beliefs and lifestyle, abetted by his doting and equally free-thinking mother, resulted in an unusual domestic environment in which his two families lived under one roof. Neither Djuna nor her brothers attended school, receiving a creative and artistic education at home. In *Ryder*, Barnes offers a largely sympathetic portrayal of her father, which celebrates his social nonconformism even though it also expresses her resentment at his constant adultery. In her later work, however, notably Nora's dream of her leering grandmother in *Nightwood*, and the family hatred and tragedy of *The Antiphon*, she would reveal a more emotionally abusive family history and the memory of sexual advances by both her father and grandmother. Angry at her father's unfaithfulness and what she perceived as her mother's bias towards her sons, Barnes certainly formed her closest family attachment with her grandmother, one that the teasingly erotic letters from Zadel to Djuna in the Barnes archive suggest may have been incestuous. In *Ryder*, Wendell's daughter Julie, the character who can be equated with Barnes herself, is described as Sophia's 'favourite child' (*R* 143).

Zadel, with her stories of her life as a journalist and her literary salon in London, was undoubtedly an influence on her granddaughter. In Barnes's fictional version of her family history, she recalls Zadel's varied interests and vibrant imagination in an image of the walls of Sophia's bedroom, onto which are repeatedly pasted pictures that fascinate her, forming a palimpsestic scrapbook of history and identity, from which no picture or clipping is ever removed:

> Sophia's wall, like the telltale rings of the oak, gave up her conditions, as anyone might have discovered an they had taken a bucket of water to it, for she never removed, she covered over. [. . .] the originals were, as she herself was, nothing erased but much submerged. (*R* 13)

She admires self-reliant women, including 'George Eliot, Brontë, Elizabeth Stanton, Ouida, the great Catherine, Beatrice Cenci, Lotta Crabtree, and the great whore of the spirit, the procuress of the dead, the madame of the Bawdy-house-of-the-Shades, the miracle worker – "Caddy-Catch-Can" ' (*R* 13). The mix is eclectic but all are marked by determination or unconventionality. One or both of these qualities is evident in each woman: the writers George Eliot and Emily Brontë (Barnes pointedly referring to the pagan-orientated Emily as *the* Brontë); leading suffragist Elizabeth Stanton; Catherine, Empress of Russia; sensation writer Ouida; Lotta Crabtree, a hugely popular nineteenth-century variety actress; and Beatrice Cenci, a young Roman noblewoman sentenced to death by the Pope in 1599 for the murder of her cruel father, whose story was turned into a verse tragedy by Percy Bysshe Shelley in 1819. 'Caddy-Catch-Can' is possibly Madame Helena Blavatsky, the Russian spiritualist and co-founder of Theosophy, who Phillip Herring suggests Zadel Barnes may have known in London.[6] The male figures pictured on the wall are more divergent in their appeal, 'men she admired for this and that' (*R* 13), but include Dante, Oscar Wilde and Savonarola, the ascetic Dominican preacher who denounced the corruption of the Medici dynasty in Florence and was excommunicated and sentenced to death for heresy in 1498. All hold the status of quasi-prophet or divine celebrity. Following down the wall from the portraits are prints of 'all she abhorred', various forms of human and animal torture, and a picture of capital punishment by pregnancy, 'the filling of the belly, known as

31

the Extreme Agony' (*R* 13), in which reproduction is again portrayed as torturous and unnatural.

Sophia is described as coming from

> a great and a humorous stock. By 'great' is meant hardy, hardy in life and hardy in death – the early Puritan. [. . .] By 'humorous' is meant ability to round out the inevitable ever-recurring meanness of life, to push the ridiculous into the very arms of the sublime. (*R* 9)

Barnes viewed the American puritan past with a consistent hatred, but, for her too, humour provided a means of relief from the adversity of human existence, and 'to push the ridiculous into the very arms of the sublime' offers a succinct summary of her constant aim in both life and literature. The strategy is epitomized in the story of the series of five chamber-pots that are ordered by Sophia when she comes of age, embellished in gold lettering with the phrases 'Needs there are many', 'Comforts are few', 'Do what you will', 'Tis no more than I do', 'Amen' (*R* 11). Ten years later, two of the pots have been broken and thus the lines 'Comforts are Few' and 'Tis no more than I do' have been lost. Shortly after, 'Do what you will' suffers a similar fate, and after another ten months 'Needs there are many'. Only 'Amen' is left, and 'Sophia looked upon this catastrophe with something of fear' (*R* 12). Representing different stages in life, the pots mark the early loss of any comfort and sense of autonomy, followed later by indifference. Man is left only with needs, which disappear when he prays for death. The theme is Barnes's black vision of existence, but the manner of telling is an example of the coexistent wit that provides the repartee to her despair and characterizes the mock-epic style of the novel.

JESUS MUNDANE

Ryder opens with the introduction of Wendell as 'Jesus Mundane', accompanied by a drawing in which he sits astride his horse on a cloud, surrounded by adoring women in puritan dress. In a parody of the Bible, the text informs the reader of his divine calling as a fleshly saviour:

Go not with fanatics who see beyond thee and thine [. . .] for such need thee not, nor see thee, nor know thy lamenting, so confounded are they with thy damnation and the damnation of thy offspring, and the multiple damnation of those multitudes that shall be of thy race begotten [. . .]. Alike are they distracted with thy salvation and the salvation of thy people. Go thou, then, to lesser men, who have for all things unfinished and uncertain, a great capacity, for these shall not repulse thee, thy physical body and thy temporal agony, thy weeping and thy laughing and thy lamenting. (*R* 3)

Wendell's role on Earth, as he imagines it, is not to conform to the religious 'fanatics' who aim for salvation through the rejection and damnation of material pleasures and the denial of the physical body, but to promote a doctrine of superabundant procreation. The prodigal son, his vain desire is to become the 'Father of All Things' (*R* 210), a philosophy that he passes on to his son Timothy. His boast is to create a race in which all aspects of beast and human will be combined and 'No heart will beat with a difference' (*R* 211), and to achieve this aim he pursues a plan of 'bedding in all beds' (*R* 211) and encouraging free love amongst all things. An underlying theme of the novel is thus the exploration of the differentiation of nature and culture, focusing on the clash between Wendell's lustiness and the society within which he lives. Barnes's perspective is ambiguous, implying support of Wendell's lifestyle as an act of resistance against an austere Protestant morality, and yet critiquing the denigration of women by his arrogant masculinity. In part his unorthodox lifestyle suggests an alternative to the social hegemony of middle-class conservatism and sexual repression, and as such Wendell is an appealing character, with an instinctive and vital approach to life, his insistence on the naturalness of sexual activity, and his recognition of female sexual desire, for example, radically denying the strict religious and moral doctrine of provincial American puritanism. At the same time, however, Wendell remains firmly entrenched within a gendered account of sexuality, in which the purpose of intercourse is procreation and women's sensual pleasure only of importance as a boost to his male vanity.

The tension between these accounts is debated in chapter eight by two unmarried sisters 'Pro and Con', whose role seems to be that of a chorus, breaking the flow of the narrative to provide commentary on Wendell's character. While Pro contemplates the possible truth of his claim that 'no woman, however fanciful, however given to speculation and to trial, to coquetry and to gorging, can be happy without his peculiar kind of collusion' (*R* 39), Con argues tartly that he 'paints a rosy picture of polygamy' only for 'the *man*' (*R* 40–41). Contemplating the choice of fleshly sexuality or spinster gentility, they decide to opt for the latter. A similar comparison pervades the discussion between Amelia, as she is about to leave for America and marriage with Wendell, and her sister Ann, who chooses to remain unmarried and live as a female companion. Despite the calm and rational arguments that are made against Wendell, however, the life of the spinster is empty and sterile when compared with the passion and vitality of his sexual activity. Pro and Con, for example, indulging in discussion of Wendell's exploits as a titillating diversion from the polite decorum of their everyday life, recall Vera and Amelia Burgson from Barnes's play *The Dove*, frustrated by their repressed desires. Barnes does briefly hint at an alternative, in the description of six women who satisfy their sexual desires amongst themselves in lesbian foreplay, 'snatching at their companions' individual herbage and soft spots' (*R* 41). With the arrival of Wendell and his 'thundering male parts' (*R* 42), however, this non-procreative sexual activity is quickly abandoned and the women instead fight each other in jealousy.

Throughout *Ryder* Barnes voices a dark underside to Wendell's philosophy of procreation by calling attention to the pain and destructiveness of childbirth. Written against the socio-political background of the birth control movement of the 1910s and 1920s, which attempted to counter disease, high maternal death rates and excessive family size, the novel reflects not only the argument for contraception by campaigners such as Margaret Sanger in the US and Marie Stopes in England, but also a cultural backlash and re-emphasis by patriarchal Western society of women's fundamental role as child-bearer. Wendell, for example, argues that free love is a natural and therefore moral act, but his continual promiscuity without any use of contraception results in the frequent pregnancies of both Amelia and Kate, and the financial burden of an ever-increasing family. By the end of the novel, when the 60-year-old Sophia is forced into begging and he attempts to economize on the household expenses by feeding the children with bread made from cow feed, his wife and mistress have little sympathy. Their long obligation to satisfy his sexual demands is now counterbalanced by Wendell's responsibility to support them and their children. Overhearing Wendell and Sophia discussing what they are to do, for example, Kate screams in fury that he has brought his troubles upon himself:

> 'I'll have my children, as many as I like, and that for you! [. . .] you've taken me, you've brought me to your house, you've bred with me, and I've got the taste.' Here she laughed. 'I've become infatuated with the flavour of motherhood; you poked it under my nose, and I've learned to like it. It makes me ill, and there's no pleasure at either end, but I'm addicted, and it's your fault, keeper of the shop, and madame of the keeper!' (*R* 170)

When he pleads to Sophia 'Mother, what does one do with nature?', even she turns away, recognizing Kate's suffering in pregnancy and responding wearily that 'A humane man would occasionally give it respite' (*R* 172).

If Barnes's relish of the humorous bawdy and romping pace of language in *Ryder* endorses sexual activity as natural and pleasurable, her representation of pregnancy as a condition that weakens the female body and can even prove fatal expresses angry support of the need for women's sexual emancipation through birth control. Chapter thirteen, 'Midwives' Lament, or the Horrid Outcome of Wendell's First Infidelity', is a brief and sombre verse that commemorates the death of one of his sexual conquests,

> Who died as women die, unequally
> Impaled upon a death that crawls within;
> For men die otherwise, of man unsheathed
> But women on a sword they scabbard to.
> And so this girl, untimely to the point,
> Pricked herself upon her son and passed
> Like any Roman bleeding on the blade –
>
> (*R* 77)

The euphemisms are unmistakably transparent and the woman dies as a result of Wendell's penetrating penis, 'pricked' by his 'sword' and 'impaled' on the child within her. Such a disaster seems impossible to prevent, however, as man is locked into a cycle of reproduction. The chapter 'Rape and Repining', for example, sets a more general context for Wendell's sexual roving. Bemoaning women's inevitable fall –

> A Girl is gone! A Girl is lost! A simple Rustic Maiden but Yesterday swung upon the Pasture Gate, with Knowledge no-where, yet is now, to-day, no better than her Mother, and her Mother's Mother before her! Soiled! Despoiled! Handled! Mauled! Rumpled! Rummaged! Ransacked! (*R* 21)

– the narrator despairingly mourns the rapid loss of virginity, venting an angry diatribe against such easy capitulation to male seduction:

> Can Hounds track her down to Original Approval: the Law frame her Maidenly again; the not-of-occurring-particular-Popish dispen-sation reset her Virginal? Can Conclaves and Hosts, Mob and Rabble, Stone her back into that sweet and lost condition? Nay, nor one Nun going down before the down going Candle, pray her Neat. (*R* 21)

The tone is exaggerated, and the chapter at first a parody of moralistic dismay at such abandoned behaviour from the liberal perspective of the 1920s. As it continues, however, the reason for the narrator's passion – which is that heterosexual coupling extends and continues the torturous existence that human beings must endure before death – becomes apparent. A similar notion of the painful mortality of mankind is found in Dr Matthew O'Connor's alternative account of the Genesis myth, in which 'Sorrow burst and the seeds fell and took root, and climbed about the stations of the cross and bore Him down to earth, and climbed on and on and bore Matthew and Nora and Jason down to earth, [. . .] and climbed on and bore their children and their children's children down to earth' (*R* 140). Wendell's philosophy of procreation, intended to endow his name with immortality, is thus ironically also associated with the death wish. 'Man is born to die', the narrator informs the woman reader, 'and we, with Fortitude, have made the

Farthest Outposts of Death a Lawful Goal, but you, in this Wanton Act, have advanced that Mark' (*R* 27). Women are thus made as responsible as Ryder himself for the perpetuation of the human race, and the chapter ends in frustration at the inevitability of male and female coupling: 'It is Spring again [. . .] It is Girls' Weather and Boys' Luck' (*R* 29).

This negative representation of the inevitability of reproduction and motherhood is immediately followed by the chapter introducing Amelia de Grier, Wendell's future wife. When Amelia is 17, her mother tells her to 'Never, never, have children', but, resigned to the futility of her warning, predicts: 'It takes a strong woman to die before she has been a fool. No one has the imagination; I did not, you will not' (*R* 32). Amelia in turn later tells her own daughter, Julie, 'Once I was safe enough and I could not let well enough alone, but must get myself in the way of doom and damnation by being natural. So take warning by my size and don't let a man touch you, for their touching never ends, and screaming oneself into a mother is no pleasure at all' (*R* 95). As she goes into labour, however, the 10-year-old Julie lies on her bed, clutching a doll to her stomach and screaming in mock childbirth. Pregnancy seems impossible to avoid, but it makes of women little other than self-destructive breeding machines. Sophia's mother, Cynthia, after years of continual child-bearing, lies on her deathbed with her fourteenth, 'a terrible suffering centre without extremities' (*R* 7).

DENYING THE FATHER

Despite Wendell's mission to become the progenitor of an entire 'Ryder' race, the novel actually constantly undercuts the patrilineal, notably through women who confound the male act of fathering and deny the otherwise inevitability of women's reproductive role. Sophia Ryder, although herself a mother, and a woman who gains the devotion of single women and appeases the jealousy of wives by demanding 'Call me mother!' (*R* 12), refuses men any status as the father of her children. Her own conception is never described, the novel stating only that 'she had hatched on every side' (*R* 9).

Moreover, contriving to remain aloof from woman's guilt and complicity in procreation, she denies having intercourse with Wendell's father, the Latin tutor John Peel, after her first fall. Telling Wendell that he was conceived in a dream in which she was visited by the spirit of Beethoven, she claims: 'You know well enough how thoroughly I hated your father. Would it be conceivable then, that I, of some mettlesome quality, should give him access to that place that so heartily complained upon the first intrusion?' (R 37). Refusing her husband's name for both herself and her children, it is thus Sophia who stands at the head of the Ryder family tree, as matriarch and the main financial provider for the family. By the age of 70, when her son has reduced his family to penury, she turns her talents to 'superbly conceived letters of beggary' (R 14), always signed 'Mother', to wealthy men that she had known in earlier days. 'Dressing in irreproachable linen, wrapping her pauper's cloak about her' (R 15), she resourcefully manages to keep the family in comfort.

Two other women, Molly Dance and Lady Bridesleep, oppose male sexual authority by directly repudiating Wendell's claim of fatherhood. As her name suggests, Molly Dance is a woman who has enjoyed sexual promiscuity as much as Wendell himself, and who has 'got her children where and when it pleased her' (R 191). Unaware of who her father is, she is as unconcerned about the fact that she does not know who the various fathers of her own children might be as she is about their illegitimacy. Wendell's masculine pride, by contrast, is bewildered by her indifference, as she asks him, 'who cares? He didn't, I don't, and the child won't have to, and that's simplification' (R 198). To 'simplify' men out of the reproductive equation is unbelievable to Wendell, however, who offers to father the next child, seemingly naïvely unaware of Molly's mocking agreement and her power to easily undercut his patriarchal authority. After intercourse he is thus confounded when she slyly teases, 'there's only one thing that might make something uncertain of this certainty' (R 199), telling him that a policeman had had the same idea two nights before. Refusing Wendell's phallocentric suggestion, moreover, that whereas his promiscuity is a divine act, her own is damned and will lead her to hell, she asserts that 'Original sin was not at all as your biographers make it [. . .] original sin was not a woman's' (*R* 197).

Lady Bridesleep, an older woman who has past her menopause, also determines to ridicule Wendell's conviction of his role as primogenitor. Like Molly Dance, Lady Bridesleep too enjoys the sensual pleasures of the sexual act, yet as a result of her sterility is able to indulge without fear of pregnancy. Realizing that Wendell is ignorant of her age, she welcomes his flatteries and knowingly allows him to seduce her. The following morning however, when Wendell asks her what they should name their child, she laughs at his presumption, replying, 'Nothing and Never [. . .] No child'. Explaining that his seed has been wasted within a barren body, she tells him that this 'non-child' proves his fallibility, and that 'On him you shall hang that part of your ambition too heavy for mortal' (*R* 211).

One other figure who stands in contrast to Wendell's virile, procreative philosophy is the homosexual Dr Matthew O'Connor, the physician who attends the pregnancies of Amelia, Kate and Molly Dance and will reappear, older, more bitter and more verbose in *Nightwood*. O'Connor's occupation as a physician places him in alliance with natural science, dealing with the physical body and its growth and degeneration. Despite thus accepting the body as animal, however, he contemplates the mortality of the body with despair. Refusing to deny the desires of his flesh, he is yet also desperate for some meaning and spiritual life beyond it, which he seeks in the rites of the Catholic Church. Unlike Wendell, who is agnostic and attempts to detach himself from the authority of the Church, O'Connor turns to the church in order to articulate as a sin at the confessional his otherwise 'unspeakable' homosexuality, and to cry in blasphemous prayer at the altar: 'who am I that I should be damned forever and forever, Amen?' (*R* 139). At his words however, he experiences a vision in which the church burns in flames around a black mass:

> The candles took root and grew and rose toward the ceiling, and bloomed and wilted and died, and the ceiling grew and mounted and bloomed and wilted and died, and came down. And the stars came out on the great pillars of the candelabrum, and slid with them and dwindled and flickered and stood once more about the

bier, the soft bodies of mourners in woolly clothing kneeling. [. . .]
The figures at the altar blurred, crossed, melted into each other;
fornication of the mass, parted and bred Death, Death's wailing child
in wax, lying in a pool of wine, mouth open for the gushing breast of
grief, pouring forth the Word in an even belt of wrath. The sacred
cow swam the shallow chancel, a garland on his brow, lowing, In
peace let him rest! The church turned upside down.'   (R 140)

The scene is one of profane spiritual inversion. Although it
upturns religious doctrine, however, it does not negate ador-
ation of, or supplication to, the mystical. As a more degenerate
O'Connor will explain in *Nightwood*, the opulent Catholicism
of an ancient Europe, rather than the austere Puritanism of
new and progressive America, holds solace for the damned in
its sensuous spirituality. For it is with the decoration of the
Catholic church, its candelabra, wine and garlands, that he
envisions a material worship and erotic ecstasy, one that
depends on the acknowledgement of faith and divinity even
within a profane communion.

MYSTICISM AND THE BEAST

Wendell spurns the Church, in jealousy over the status of God
as the supreme father. Denying the spirit, he justifies his
doctrine of polygamy by identifying his actions with those of
the animal world, claiming that his promiscuity is natural and
bestial. He is sensitive to the natural world and recognizes an
affinity with the animal in the sensual and instinctive aspects
of the human organism; man's beating heart and physical
needs and desires. In the verse summary of the novel in
chapter ten, 'The Occupations of Wendell', for example, he
questions the difference between his own instinctive desires
and those of the animal world:

> Eft Wendell pondered, and he say him 'Sooth!
> What is this swims like dregs within the truth
> That animal and man be set apart?
> I hear not much difference in the heart
> That beats soft and constant under hide,
> And this same hammer ticking in my side!'

(R 61)

Although the equation is select and ultimately superficial, Wendell associating himself predominantly with the stud, in a hierarchy of beasts in which women are viewed merely as breeding stock for his valuable seed, he nevertheless disrupts the binary divisions of nature/culture and beast/human by refusing to distinguish himself from nature or to differentiate his family from his animals.

In *Beasts of the Modern Imagination* (1985), Margot Norris identifies a brief period, lasting from roughly the last decade of the nineteenth century to the 1930s, in which the cultural and biological uncertainty that resulted from evolutionary theory brought about a new fascination with the instinctual and the bodily, temporarily binding what she describes as 'the great cleft produced in our human being by the repression of the animal and the living body'.[7] This perspective, the blurring of the categories of man and beast, is a marked feature of Barnes's work. A primary source for *Ryder*, for example, was *L'Imagerie imaginaire* (1926), a collection of images of human-animal hybrids from the fifteenth century in which animals take on human roles and vice versa in an upturned hierarchy of the human and bestial, and a carnivalesque prediction of the nineteenth-century Darwinian collapse of man and animal that shook the anthropocentric assumptions of Western civilization. Images of animal and human morphology occur, moreover, in Barnes's Beardsleyesque illustrations for the poems of *The Book of Repulsive Women*, and continue in *Nightwood*, *The Antiphon* and the unfinished *Creatures in an Alphabet*.

What fascinates Barnes in all these texts, including *Ryder*, is the animal heritage within man's prehistory, the vestiges of animal spirit that remain embedded within the human memory and influence a connection and mutual recognition between man and beast, 'something recognized, forgotten, and yet insistent still in affects, instincts and dreams, like a faint nostalgia for our own infantile and presocial past'.[8] Wendell does not fully realize this connection until the closing chapter of the book. When, after capitulating to social demand and telling Amelia that he has chosen Kate over her as his wife, he escapes the house and sits helplessly pondering the future in a field, the animals surround him:

41

And everything and its shape became clear in the dark, by tens and tens they ranged, and lifted their lids and looked at him; in the air and in the trees and on the earth and from under the earth, and regarded him long, and he forbore to hide his face. They seemed close ranged, and now they seemed far ranged, and they moved now near, now far, as a wave comes and goes, and they lifted their lids and regarded him, and spoke not in their many tongues, and they went a far way, and there was a little rest, and they came close, and there was none. (R 242)

For Barnes then it is not so much in his carnal instincts that Wendell approaches true connection with the animal, but in this recognition of their dumb appeal when he has surrendered them to the forces of social authority and convention.

Ryder portrays a semi-mystical, cultural memory of the bestial that prefigures that of Robin Vote in *Nightwood*, perhaps one reason for Barnes's dedication of the novel to Thelma Wood. In the story of Beast Thingumbob, for example, which Wendell tells to his children Julie and Timothy, the natural world is presented as a realm of folklore or fairytale, the Beast himself being part bird, part lion and part ram. The Beast falls in love with a woman-like creature with no face, ten breasts, and hoofs instead of feet. The female beast has lived for hundreds of years without love but is 'not virgin as other women are' (R 119), by which Wendell seems to mean that she has been contented with her single existence, as although 'she had a greater share than any mortal woman could bear or possibly see to put up with, [. . .] to her the putting up was no great business' (R 120). Now, however, 'fettered to the earth for a season of harvesting, after which she was to return to the gods' (R 119), her time has come for sexual consummation. The physical act of love is her ultimate purpose on earth but will result in her death, and she calls the Beast to her, telling him 'I shall die beneath you, yet from my body you shall garner ten sons' (R 121).

The story is in part a further example of Wendell's own idealistic vision of himself as a natural beast with a spiritual purpose to deliver women from the asexual state of virginity, and a commentary on the destructive effects of his constant siring on his wife and mistress. It is also a mystical allegory of the fertility cycle of birth and death, however, that hints at an earlier, prehistorical state in which the cycle of time has no relevance. The story confounds not only social and religious but also evolutionary hypotheses of man identity and genealogy, and the illustration that accompanies the story, which depicts Beast Thingumbob in mourning next to his dying mate, was significantly one of those censored from the original edition for its 'unnatural' subject matter.

'And what does it mean?' asks Timothy as he contemplates the story of Beast Thingumbob. A similar question was silently posed by *Ryder*'s appreciative but perplexed contemporary reviewers, who drew attention to the novel's broad humour and presentation of a grotesque comedy of the human body, but avoided commentary on plot and meaning by focusing on Barnes's deft parodies of her bawdy influences, which by general consent were regarded as Rabelais, Sterne, Fielding and Joyce. With the colourful characters, witty eighteenth-century dialogue and complex formal style of *Ryder*, Barnes certainly proclaimed her status within Paris-based modernism, yet perhaps this very association also resulted in a simultaneous diversion of attention from the gender perspective of her narrative, her attempt to write the *'female* Tom Jones'. On the republication of *Ryder* in 1980, the *San Francisco Review of Books* commented:

> Perhaps language, however elaborately deployed, cannot gain human beings, particularly women, much purchase against their sexuality, against whatever combination of desire, obsession, trust, and despair binds them to torment at the hands of another. It may, however, provide a temporary reprieve, especially when the readily available alternative – isolation and sterility – begins to exert its fascination.[9]

The reviewer had the benefit of speaking from hindsight. Three months after the publication of *Ryder*, Barnes's pseudonymous *Ladies Almanack* became available on the streets of Paris, a chapbook in which language again battles against male authority, through the teasing tongue of a lesbian saint.

3

Sapphic Satire: *Ladies Almanack*

'Paris has always seemed to me the only city where you can live and express yourself as you please'[1]

Ladies Almanack (1928) is a companion piece to *Ryder*, written in the same year but moving from Barnes's family history to the social scene of her contemporary Paris, and from the patriarchal lusts of Wendell Ryder to the lesbian dalliances of Dame Evangeline Musset. It claims to be 'the book all ladies should carry' (*LA* 5), and is described on the title page as 'showing their Signs and their tides; their Moons and their Changes; the Seasons as it is with them; their Eclipses and Equinoxes; as well as a full Record of diurnal and nocturnal distempers' (*LA* 3). Written at the request of Natalie Barney, it presents a quasi-biography of Dame Musset, self-styled saviour of lesbians, who is based on Barney herself and the sapphic salon she held at her house at 20, rue Jacob. Privately published by Robert McAlmon for Contact Press, with 1,050 copies printed by Darantière Press, the first fifty hand-coloured by Barnes, Tylia Perlmutter and Mina Loy's daughter Fabienne, it quickly became an underground novelty, hawked by Barnes on the streets of Paris. Its style mimics Robert Burton's *Anatomy of Melancholy* (1621), one of Barnes's favourite books, and the tone is similar to that of *Ryder*, although, derived more from the comedy of manners of the Restoration, its language is more evasive and coded, and the bawdy lustiness less overt, perhaps in response to the threat of the same censorship that had afflicted the previous work. It was probably for this reason that Barnes avoided using her own

44

name as author and attributed the book instead to a 'Lady of Fashion', a pseudonym that suited the generic style of the almanac but that also protected her from explicit connection with its sexual subject.

Since its first official publication in 1972, *Ladies Almanack* has become a contentious text within feminist critical debate, described as a 'Sapphic manifesto' but also as a vicious satire that subscribes to a 'demeaning' and 'reductionist' account of lesbian identity.[2] Dispute has tended to centre on the question of Barnes's own allegiance to hetero- or homosexuality, which is as ambiguous in the *Almanack* as it was in her own life, and her long dismissal of the novel as simply 'a jollity', written for the pleasure of Natalie Barney and to amuse Thelma Wood while she was in hospital. Her refusal to republish it for over forty years has been interpreted as indication of a denial of her own fluid sexuality that borders on homophobia. Barnes's foreword to the 1972 republication, however, openly declares *Ladies Almanack* to be an imaginative portrayal of lesbian eroticism. Moreover, claiming the specific literary purpose of presenting an alternative account of homosexuality to that of Proust's *Sodom et Gomorrhe* (1922), she describes the book as:

> Neap-tide to the Proustian chronicle, gleanings from the shore of Mytilene, glimpses of its novitiates, its rising 'saints' and 'priest-esses,' and thereon to such aptitude and insouciance that they took to gaming and to swapping that 'other' of the mystery, the anomaly that calls the hidden name that, affronted, eats its shadow.[3]

Both Barnes and Barney disagreed with Proust's representation of lesbianism. The *Almanack* does not define lesbianism in terms of the sins of the ancient 'cities of the plain', as Proust had done when he described Sodom and Gomorrah as surviving within the homosexual culture of urban modernity. Instead it turns to the classical Greek city of Mytilene, on the island of Lesbos, home of the lesbian poet Sappho. Barnes also rewrites another influential lesbian text, Radclyffe Hall's *The Well of Loneliness*, published in July of the same year and which depicted Natalie Barney as Valerie Seymour. Hall's novel attempted an 'apology' for female homosexual identity that drew heavily on the sexological theory of 'inversion', which constructs the homosexual as a natural, biological mistake, and despite its euphemistic portrayal of lesbianism, along with the scientific support of an introduction by Havelock Ellis, was banned for obscenity in England after a notorious trial.

Certainly the esotericism of *Ladies Almanack*, a pastiche in which narrative passages intersect with poetry, pagan lore and amazonian philosophy – all of which constantly contradict themselves, are pervaded by obscure archaic language, and frequently disregard the grammatical rules of sentence structure – could perhaps check censorship in a way that the stylistically conservative, and thus more accessible, *Well of Loneliness* could not. Yet Barnes also takes issue with Hall's subscription to the discourse of 'inversion' and, in contrast to Hall's unhappy and ashamed protagonist Stephen Gordon, presents lesbianism as a condition which women are variously born or converted to, or come to choose. In *The Book of Repulsive Women* Barnes had portrayed female sexuality as hideous and perverse, and in *Ryder* as destroyed by women's function as physical reproduction machines for Wendell Ryder's abundant male seed. *Ladies Almanack* celebrates the lesbian's resistance to patriarchal demand in her refusal to reproduce, and the pleasures available to the female body when undefiled by the pain of male intrusion and possession. In the world of *Ladies Almanack*, it is heterosexuality that causes the degeneration and ageing of the female body, and lesbianism that is the state of pure and virginal womanhood. Rejecting conventional understanding of both textuality and sexuality, Barnes writes a 'queer poetics' of the female body. *Ladies Almanack* is at once a lively roman à clef, a metatext of the sexual and textual politics of Sapphic modernism, and a celestial map that articulates through teasing commentary and verbal play the workings, sensations and desires of the female body across time.

SODOM AND GOMORRAH OR MYTILENE?

Dame Evangeline Musset, the reader is told in the preface to *Ladies Almanack*, 'had been developed in the Womb of her most gentle Mother to be a Boy', and 'when therefore, she came forth an Inch or so less than this, she paid no Heed to the Error' (*LA* 7). From these origins she dedicates her life to liberation and recruitment of lesbian women from the confines of heterosexual culture. The frontispiece depicts her 'stepping out upon that exceedingly thin ice to which it has pleased God, more and more, to call frail woman', extending her pole to the reach of several women who have fallen through and are at various stages of drowning in the cold and engulfing waters of heterosexist social opinion. The lesbian community she develops is one in which women are encouraged to enjoy their sexuality and not feel self-hatred at their difference from the prescribed norm of heterosexuality. Her model, Natalie Clifford Barney, was an American heiress who, after the death of her father in 1902, lived permanently in Paris. In 1904 she made her first visit to Lesbos, the island where Sappho was born, returning to recreate a sapphic world in contemporary Paris. In contrast to the nineteenth-century symbolist and decadent representation of the lesbian as a figure of vice and damnation, Barney celebrated female homosexuality as healthy desire, love expressed through the pleasures of the body. The body of the lesbian, far from perverse, was for Barney the female body that was whole and pure, and that remained in possession of itself, not violated by the demands of childbirth. Her sapphic vision imagined the lesbian as sensual and feminine, existing within a premodern, Arcadian environment.

Barney's Parisian 'Mytilene' was a semi-private space in which women could indulge in sapphic flirtation, but also an aesthetic community in which she sought to support both male and female writers and artists. Guests included Colette, Gertrude Stein, Isadora Duncan, Ford Madox Ford, Ezra Pound, Ernest Hemingway, Jean Cocteau and even Greta Garbo. Attendance was restricted to an elite group of aristocrats, heiresses, artists and intellectuals. As Shari Benstock describes,

> Barney was aristocratic in her efforts to create a privileged women's culture in Paris, committing herself only to women of breeding or of great artistic talent. She played the part of an eighteenth century aristocrat, enforcing a *droit de seigneur* that insured her privilege and sexual freedom.[4]

47

Barnes met Natalie Barney shortly after her first arrival in Paris, probably in 1922, became a regular member of her salon, and received her intermittent financial support, rather ungraciously, throughout her life. In 1927, the year before *Ladies Almanack*, Barney initiated her *Académie des femmes*, a series of salon evenings with the specific purpose of promoting women writers (Barnes, the poet Mina Loy and Gertrude Stein were all granted sessions in their honour). Outside the formality of the Académie sessions, however, the atmosphere of the more private gatherings of Barney's immediate friends at the rue Jacob was lively and teasing, and it is this gregarious environment that *Ladies Almanack* captures and lampoons.

Barnes was irked by her dependency on Barney, however, and also on Peggy Guggenheim, for economic patronage, and although *Ladies Almanack* was written partly to please a friend and important benefactor, and as a spoof on lesbianism for a select readership familiar with its sexual slang and euphemisms, it was also an exercise in modernist formal experimentation and avant-garde self-promotion. For despite the recent tendency to locate Barnes within a new modernist canon of women writers and female support networks – the somewhat distorted result of the efforts of feminist revisionist critics to reclaim her reputation from the obscurity to which it had fallen within institutionalized modernist studies – in the 1920s and 1930s she was widely regarded as a writer who could rival the status of almost any other in Paris, and the only figure comparable to James Joyce. Janet Flanner, the sophisticated, cosmopolitan and androgynous 'Genêt' who wrote a fortnightly column, 'Letter from Paris', for the *New Yorker* from 1925 to 1971, recalled in the introduction to her collection *Paris Was Yesterday*, that,

> Djuna Barnes was the most important woman writer we had in Paris. [. . .] I was devoted to Djuna and she was quite fond of me, too, in her superior way. She wrote a chapbook called *The Little Ladies' Almanac*, and illustrated it boldly. It was a take-off of many ladies in the American colony, published privately, I think by Natalie Barney, *doyenne* of the Left Bank, who appeared in it as a leading character under the guise of Dame Musset. I was one of a pair of journalists called Nip and Tuck.[5]

48

As a respected writer publishing regularly in the *Little Review* and *transatlantic review*, Barnes moved between the spaces of Barney's salon and Anglo-American modernism, associating herself professionally with the latter. Apart from Barney and Mina Loy, one of Barnes's closest friends from Greenwich Village, who appears in the almanac as Patience Scalpel, she seems to have regarded other members of the group with a degree of artistic superiority. Barney's freedom to acknowledge her sexual interest in women and ignore the conventions of heterosexist society was largely the result of her considerable wealth and thus financial independence, along with a robust obliviousness to homophobia and seemingly complete absence of any feelings of self-doubt or abnormality. As Elyse Blankley notes, however, 'Few lesbian women were able to live as bravely as Natalie Barney; most, in fact, grew weary of playing the sex-role game according to Paris's rules – rules more painful because masked by many illusory freedoms'.[6] Barnes recognized the social limits and emotional costs of the Barney lifestyle, and although she presents Dame Musset as a promiscuous but generally positive figure in *Ladies Almanack*, she also satirizes the coterie nature and elitist precocity of her circle of acolytes as comfortable and leisured women who indulge in teasing discussions and egocentric squabbles.

In ironic contrast to Wendell, the 'Jesus Mundane' of *Ryder* who energetically champions a philosophy of free love and procreation, Dame Musset, or 'Saint Evangeline', equally zealously seeks to convert women to the non-procreative love and purely libidinal sexual enjoyment of the lesbian. His 'immaculate conception' by Beethoven is balanced by her inception by the twelve angels of the zodiac. Whereas Wendell is associated with the natural world of his farm and the beasts, Dame Musset lives within the artifice of the city, her tended garden and the celestial world of the heavens, the immediate implication being that the lesbian is at once more artificial and more civilized than the heterosexual. Both recognize that women are just as subject to sexual passions as men, although Wendell manipulates this for the dissemination of his seed, whereas Musset sets out to provide women with physical pleasure without the consequences of physical pain. Euphemistically described as 'one Grande Red Cross for the Pursuance, the Relief, and the Distraction, of such Girls as in their Hinder Parts, and their Fore Parts, and in whatsoever Parts did suffer them most, lamentably Cruelly' (*LA* 6), she is an expert in the provision of the female orgasm, her skill in 'the Consolation every woman has at her Finger Tips, or at the very Hang of her Tongue' (*LA* 6) adequately compensating for Wendell's active member.

Through an association of puns, Barnes conflates here the sexual and textual acts of lesbianism, the finger and tongue corresponding to the writing and speaking of the love of woman for woman. Dame Musset not only represents Barney's promotion of both sapphic love and sapphic modernism, but also provides a comment on Barnes's own production of a language of female love. The months of February and July both contain accounts of the lesbian text, the first a love-letter, presumably by Dame Musset or the narrator herself, and the second an attack on the sickly rhetoric used in the typical letters of female lovers. The writer of the February letter describes woman as the subject of a long tradition of literary and philosophical representation, 'a much Thumbed Mystery and a Maze' (*LA* 15), worries that nothing new can be said and finally decides that 'Fancy is my only Craft' (*LA* 17). In the July section the narrator ridicules the effusive romantic twittering of one woman to another and bemoans its lack of poetic value and stylistic discipline. Far from a language that is 'as clipped of Foliage as a British Hedge' (*LA* 42), the words of female lovers are said to revolve around such nicknames as 'Honey Lou' or 'Snooky dear' (*LA* 43). 'Nay . . . . . . I cannot write it! It is worse than this!', the narrator despairs, 'more saccharine, more lamentable, more gruesomely unmindful of Reason or Sense, to say nothing of Humor' (*LA* 46). There seems no middle ground, she complains, between the representation of lesbianism by society as grotesque and degenerate, and the covert language of female lovers that is euphemized into syrupy trivia: 'One sickens the Gorge and the other the Heart' (*LA* 46).

Barnes certainly establishes her own lesbian vocabulary, also euphemistic but gleaned from the more colourful colloquialisms of the medieval, Shakespearean and eighteenth-century past: women are described as 'Babes', 'sluts', 'baggage' and

'Jade', lesbian lovers as 'branch-to-branch', 'Womb-to-Womb' and 'braid-to-braid', the female genitalia as 'the garden of Venus' and the female orgasm as 'to bring to a certainty', 'to thaw', 'to floor', 'a beautitude'. Within everyday speech, however, the voice of female homosexuality has been silenced, Barnes seems to imply, and as yet has found no language with which to articulate herself: 'It would loom the bigger if stripped of its Jangle, but no, drugged such must go. As foggy as a Mere, as drenched as a Pump; twittering so loud upon the Wire that one cannot hear the Message. And yet!' (*LA* 46). The final exclamation suggests the possibility of an alternative, of which the February letter and the text of *Ladies Almanack* itself are perhaps examples.

LESBIAN IDENTITIES

Although *Ladies Almanack* reveals an obvious sympathy for the lesbian imagination, Barnes's detached and ironic narratorial stance, emphasized by her asides to the reader, suggests that she observes the sapphic sexual play it represents from the position of an outsider, refusing to position herself as either amongst or against Dame Musset's lesbian following. From one viewpoint the text constructs a lesbian consciousness, written as the lifetime diary of Dame Musset in which she records both events and conversations and her own poetic and philosophical musings. Natalie Barney certainly regarded it as a celebration of female homosexuality and a useful tool for the Musset-style conversion of women, writing in a letter to Richard Aldington that 'All ladies fit to figure in such an almanack should of course be eager to have a copy, and all gentlemen disapproving of them. Then the public might, with a little judicious treatment, include those lingering on the border of such islands and those eager to be ferried across'.[7] From another perspective, however, Barnes's depictions of lesbian sexuality reproduce the stereotypes of social, psychological and medical discourse.

Little has been gained by recourse to Barnes's elusive biography. The fluidity of her own sexuality has proved problematic for feminist critics who attempt to appropriate her

51

as a lesbian role model and dichotomize sexual identity between 'homo' and 'hetero' polarities. It has been too easy to respond to her blunt statement to Andrew Field, 'I'm not a lesbian, I just loved Thelma', with an 'objective' scholarly superiority that assumes defensiveness and evasion on Barnes's part. She did love Thelma, and admitted to it, but her close emotional relationships with a number of men both before and after their eight-year relationship, including Putzi Hanfstaengl, Courtenay Lemon, Charles Henri Ford and Peter Neagoe, suggest a flexible bisexuality rather than fixed lesbianism. Moreover, changing theories of sexuality, and divergences even within sexological understanding of 'inversion', result in a need to recognize early twentieth-century notions of the lesbian as constructed from a number of historically and culturally inscribed perspectives and identities.

Despite the emerging psycho-medical discourses of the late nineteenth century, through which homosexuality and transvestism became discussed and defined terms, no specific theory of female homosexuality was advanced until the beginning of the twentieth century. Jeffrey Weeks, for example, notes that 'lesbian identity was much less clearly defined, and the lesbian subculture [. . .] minimal in comparison with the male, and even more upper class or literary', although by the late 1920s when Barnes was writing *Ladies Almanack*, the cultural identity of the lesbian had become more prominent, at least among professional women.[8]

Various feminist critics have analysed the affinities to decadent culture and dandyish appearance of the Barney circle as a means of expression and signification of female homosexuality in a period when only male models were available, but which nevertheless utilized such categorizations for a lesbian counter-discourse.[9] Dame Musset's complaint in May that lesbianism has become stylized into a fashionable modern chic, however, no longer radical and therefore rather pointless, suggests that both Barney and Barnes regarded the ostentatious display of lesbianism through expensive sartorial style, such as that exhibited by Radclyffe Hall, with a degree of cynicism: 'in my day I was a Pioneer and a Menace, it was not then as it is now, *chic* and pointless to a degree, but as daring as a Crusade [. . .] What joy has the missionary [. . .] when all the Heathen greet her with Glory Halleluja ! before she opens her Mouth, and with an Amen ! before she shuts it' (*LA* 34). Lesbianism has become part of eccentric, bohemian unconventionality, to the point that even the heterosexual Patience Scalpel, usually 'so curing to the Wound', begins to 'hint, then aver, and finally boast that she herself, though all Thumbs at the business and an Amateur, never having gone to so much as a Noselength into the Matter, could mean as much to a Woman as another' (*LA* 50). Barnes's expression of female sexuality, both textual and personal, was I suggest more ambivalent and more complex. Stubbornly resenting and denying essentialist categorizations, Barnes resisted and transgressed the dualisms of what Monique Wittig describes as society's 'straight thinking'. To read the *Almanack* as a lesbian novel is thus to delimit the very disruption that it performs in refusing sexual polarization.

The sharp and witty tongue of the 'Lady of Fashion' often resembles that of Patience Scalpel, and both are observers of Dame Musset's lesbian group. Whereas Patience declares her heterosexual experiences, however, the narrator reveals no sexual preference and remains aloof. Patience Scalpel, the reader is told, 'belongs to this Almanack for one Reason only, that from Beginning to End, Top to Bottom, inside and out, she could not understand Women and their Ways' (*LA* 11), 'Women' being the term which Barnes euphemistically employs to denote 'lesbian'. Her role is partly to stand in contrast to Dame Musset as the one heterosexual woman in the book, yet although she provides an outspoken voice against lesbianism, 'as cutting in its Derision as a surgical Instrument' (*LA* 12), she also accepts and associates with Dame Musset's entourage.

Loy was ten years older than Barnes, a celebrated avant-garde poet who had been hailed by the New York press as the archetypal 'new woman' on her arrival from Europe in 1917. She was firmly non-lesbian yet, like Barnes, rejected the authority of heterosexuality as an oppressive social standard. Married twice, by the 1920s she had renounced romantic liaisons, remaining faithful to her second husband, the writer and boxer Arthur Cravan, with whom she had been together for less than two years before he mysteriously disappeared during a visit to Mexico in 1918, shortly before the birth of their daughter Fabienne. Patience Scalpel, coldly unemotional, who considers herself rather old and wise, appears to regard sexual intercourse with men as a painful and irksome experience that women require simply for the transcendental creative act of reproduction, and who thus completely fails to comprehend the love play of Dame Musset's 'Girls', is a gently satiric representation of Loy's presence within the sapphic community of Barney's salon. Loy as modernist poet, however, was also an aesthetic influence on Barnes's text, the pagan almanac with its female zodiac paralleling Loy's own focus on the moon as icon of female creativity. Scalpel is described as musing with 'Starry Eyes aloft' (*LA* 13), perhaps an allusion to the poems of *Lunar Baedecker* (1923) that continually refer to the moon and the infinity of the heavens, and reach toward a cosmic illumination and faith that is at once sacred and profane, spiritual and erotic. Natalie Barney described her as 'our guide to the moon'.

Ladies Almanack offers a similarly celestial guide to the loves and pleasure of the female body. Almanacs traditionally register the days, months and seasons of the year, recording feast and saint days, and astrological movements, defining time as at once linear and cyclical. The narrative of *Ladies Almanack* is correspondingly relayed across one calendar year, which corresponds to the one-hundred-year life of Dame Musset. In the paranormal world of *Ladies Almanack*, Evangeline is born in January, is 30 by June and dies in December aged 99, when she is elevated to the status of sainthood. The almanac also maps onto the annual cycle a mythic chronicle of womanhood through seasonal philosophies, illustrations from the zodiac, and songs and tales from ancient folklore. Lesbianism is defined as a mystic culture by both the almanac in general and by Dame Musset's circle, who regard themselves as a pagan sisterhood. Nip and Tuck, for example, who act as Dame Musset's winged messengers, rush to inform her when they find a suffering woman and potential noviciate lost in the city:

'We come', said they 'to let you know there is a Flall loose in the Town who is crying from Corner to Niche, in that lamenting Herculean Voice that sounds to us like a Sister lost, for certainly it

54

is not the Whine of Motherhood, but a more mystic, sodden Sighing. So it seems to us, as Members of the Sect, we should deliver to you this piece of information, that you may repair what has never been damaged.'

'It shall be done, and done most wily well,' said the Dame, buckling on her Four-in-hand, and clapping her Busby athwart her roguish Knee, 'Where was she last seen, and which way going?' (*LA* 31)

The lost girl who has 'never been damaged' is presumably a virgin, about to be rescued into Dame Musset's lesbian sect. Although Dame Musset regards her own homosexuality as innate, such pursuing and conversion of other women to her 'faith' implies that this is not necessarily the case and, moreover, that sexual preference can be a matter of choice. Other caricatures include Doll Furious, a portrait of Oscar Wilde's niece Dolly Wilde; Cynic Sal, Barney's lover Romaine Brooks; and Lady Buck-and-Balk and Tilly-Tweed-in-Blood, based on Lady Una Trowbridge and Radclyffe Hall. Each of these is a different manifestation of lesbian identity. Tilly-Tweed-in-Blood enters only briefly into the narrative, but it is Hall's belief in 'the third sex' of the invert, the 'manly' female who combines male strength and logic with the degenerate characteristics of a hypersensitive temperament and self-reproach, that Barnes opposes throughout the almanac. Flanner notes that 'The Paris Latin Quarter denizens first met her at a tea (with wonderful cucumber sandwiches) at Miss Natalie Barney's, heavily attended, since *The Well of Loneliness* had aroused a great deal of curiosity, if very little admiration as a literary or psychological study'. Flanner's assessment, which registers the seemingly general feeling in modernist circles that the novel was psychologically amateurish and artistically mediocre, continues:

As I recall, her whole analysis was false and based upon the fact that the heroine's mother, when expecting her, had hoped for a baby boy, which as a daughter, Miss Hall interpreted literally. This rather innocent and confused book was the first of the Sapphic interpretations in modern life.[10]

Barnes draws a direct parallel with *The Well of Loneliness* in the relatively conventional narrative of her preface to *Ladies*

Almanack, which describes Dame Musset's birth and child-hood, and explains that her lesbianism results from the fact that her mother had wanted her to be a boy. The parody continues as Evangeline's father is introduced pacing his library, aware of her difference from other women and perceiving in her 'most fatherly sentiments' (*LA* 8), just as Sir Philip Gordon recognizes his daughter's 'inversion' in Hall's novel. Dame Musset, however, unlike Stephen Gordon, is never confused or ashamed by her lesbianism, asserting to her father that she should in fact be praised for fulfilling his desire for a son:

> 'Thou, good Governor, wast expecting a Son when you lay atop of your Choosing, why then be so mortal wounded when you perceive that you have your Wish? Am I not doing after your very Desire, and is it not the more commendable, seeing that I do it without the Tools for the Trade, and yet nothing com-plain?' (*LA* 8).

From this point on, Barnes diverges dramatically from Hall, in a virtuoso performance of modernist experimentalism that rejects the theory of the female invert as a man born into a woman's body, instead emphasizing the womanly body and pleasures of the lesbian. Again like Natalie Barney, who was renowned for her countless lovers, Dame Musset's devotions are rarely constant, and she moves swiftly and casually from Doll Furious to Bouncing Bess to Cynic Sal, as well as presumably seducing her ever increasing number of 'converts'. Hall's acceptance of a heterosexual model for same-sex rela-tionships, by contrast, is dryly mocked in Lady Buck-and-Balk and Tilly-Tweed-in-Blood's adoption of masculine style dress, and their call for the legalization of same-sex marriage. For their belief in moral judgement within female love, 'a Law as binding upon her as another, that Alimony might be Collected; and that Straying be nipped in the Bud' (*LA* 20–21), in contrast to Barney's nonchalant ethic of free love, supports a concept of monogamy and possession that seems little different from the heterosexual marriage contract.

'The very Condition of Women', states the narrator in September, 'is so subject to Hazard, so complex, and so grievous, that to place her at one Moment is but to displace her

56

at the next' (*LA* 55). Through life, as through each month, woman is subject to 'Tides and Moons' and her nature is thus fluid, subject to ebb, flow and change. *Ladies Almanack* argues for a diversity of positions between the essentialist lesbianism of Musset and the heterosexuality of Patience Scalpel, from the lustful physicality of Doll Furious, to the dandyish cross-dressing of Cynic Sal and the intellectual sterility of Bouncing Bess. Moreover, in various contradictory theories of female and lesbian identity, Barnes creates parodic and extremely humorous exaggerations of the doctrines of religion, evolution, sexology and psychoanalysis, the dominant discourses in the shaping of post-Enlightenment society and thinking that were her common targets. In *Nightwood* they would be attacked as combined forces in the oppression of all that was different or 'unnatural'. In *Ladies Almanack*, however, she goes little further than pointing up their collusion as grand narratives of social and sexual identity, and wittily rewriting them into parables of the origins of female love.

Dame Musset's birth, as we have seen, is described from a sexological perspective, although Musset herself also refers to, and rejects, the psychoanalytic theory of castration and its phallocentric hypothesis that defines women by their lack of the penis. In an ironic and comical passage in which her unladylike habit of riding her horse astride rather than side-saddle, and the subsequent jolting of her anatomy, is said to make her 'hour by hour, less womanly', she argues however that 'never [. . .] has that Greek Mystery occurred to me, which is known as the Dashing out of the Testicles, and all that goes with it!' (*LA* 7). The narrator elucidates this as an event 'said to have happened to a Byzantine Baggage of the Trojan Period, more to her Surprise than her Pleasure', and another origin myth of the manly woman, commenting that 'it is an agreeable Circumstance that the Ages thought fit to hand down this Miracle, for Hope springs eternal to the human Breast' (*LA* 7). Psychoanalytic and sexological case stories are thus trivialized and set against each other as equally legitimate and equally ridiculous accounts of lesbian identity.

In two extended sections in the October entry, Barnes compares imaginative biblical and anthropological versions of the beginnings and history of lesbianism. The month of

October opens in Eden, a pre-gendered world in which 'woman' has not yet been defined as a separate identity from either beast or man. She is 'atune to every Adder, every Lion, every Tiger, every Wood thing, every Water-Wight, every Sky-wanderer' (*LA* 61), and 'still rhymed to the wild Rib that had made her' (*LA* 61). Following her 'impudent' (*LA* 62) tasting of the apple of knowledge, and the subsequent Fall, she is corrupted into womanhood as the sexual partner of man. As the generations pass, however, she becomes increasingly dissatisfied and sick, no longer desiring either man or motherhood and longing for something to break her sterility. In the world of *Ladies Almanack* it is heterosexuality that is a barren state, and lesbianism that allows for the pleasures and the bloom of female desire. It is at this point that the original story ends and 'woman', now personified as Daisy Downpour and living in Paris, sets eyes on Dame Musset and watches her from her apartment window across the ages, in part becoming a character in the novel in her own right, a strange figure of whom Dame Musset is afraid.

Paralleling the Eden myth, the next section is a parody of the evolution story from 'the Hap-hour of the World, when whelks whispered in the brink of the Night, rocked in the Cradle of Time's Ditch [. . .] until some billion of improving Years later, having toiled for the worse, and having made a stink of Advancement, became Queen-Man and King-Woman' (*LA* 69). The meanings of these passages are obscure, but their preoccupation with a state of origin that is instinctive and genderless, and exists before the beginning of time, prefigures the shadows of primitive cultural memory embodied by Robin Vote in *Nightwood*. The month of October ends with a third variant on the creation of the lesbian, a witch's brew concocted from mare's milk, the insides of a goat, 'the Stews of Secret Greek Broth' and 'some Rennet of Lesbos' (*LA* 72). The discourses of religion and evolution, like those of sexual and psychoanalytic science, are satirized by being turned into absurd riddles and compared with an old wives' tale.

Ladies Almanack offers its own lesbian creation myth in the March account of Dame Musset's astrological conception, which provides an alternative to the original 'inversion' story of her birth:

This is the part about Heaven that has never been told. After the Fall of Satan (and as he fell, Lucifer uttered a loud Cry, heard from one end of forever-and-no-end to the other) all the Angels, Aries, Taurus, Gemini, Cancer, Leo, Virgo, Libra, Scorpio, Sagittarius, Capricornus, Aquarius, Pisces, all, all gathered together, so close that they were not recognizable, one from the other. And not nine months later, there was heard under the Dome of Heaven a great Crowing, and from the Midst, an Egg, as incredible as a thing forgotten, fell to Earth, and striking, split and hatched, [. . .] And this was the first Woman born with a Difference. (*LA* 25–6)

Through the figure of Dame Musset, Barnes refuses to define lesbianism as either a biological or culturally produced state, denying any single theoretical discourse applicable to all forms of lesbian identity. When she dies in December, her role as lesbian missionary apparently no longer necessary, her funeral is celebrated by 'many Mourners of many Races and many Tempers', according to her wish that 'as they loved me differently in Life so I would have them plan differently for me in Death' (*LA* 82). The various profane and religious ceremonies culminate in the burning of her body on a pyre, where all is burned to ash except her tongue, on which the flame continues to flicker. *Ladies Almanack* is a self-conscious account and critical engagement with the figure of the lesbian. Exploring, questioning and manipulating medical, literary and popular perceptions of female sexuality, the almanac questions the Proustian representation of homosexuality as depravity, and supports, even though mildly mocking, Barney's construction of a sapphic sexual community. The tongue is Dame Musset's miracle, providing a final sexual communion for her followers and symbolizing her legacy for a lesbian literary consciousness.

4

Barnes's Hilarious Sorrow: *Nightwood*

' "Nightwood," like that, one word, it makes it sound like night-shade, poison and night and forest, and tough, in the meaty sense, and simple yet singular . . . Do you like it?'[1]

Nightwood was Djuna Barnes's magnum opus, a personal exorcism of her love for Thelma Wood, testimonial to the dying embers of an expatriate modernism, and hallucinatory depiction of the fragmented arena that was 1930s Europe. It was also an expression of her belief in the blood-consciousness of the human beast, a treatise on good and evil, and gargantuan black comedy. For some the grim drama of love and desire, pervaded by the mysticism of the pagan and the occult, the miasma of evil, the odour of decay and over-ripening, and the degenerate twilight of European civilization, suggested a long outmoded atmosphere of exoticized fin-de-siècle angst. Philip Rahv, for example, writing in the *New Masses*, complained that Barnes had 'merely exploited perversion to create an atmosphere of general mystification and psychic disorder that will permit her to transcend reality and make plausible a certain modernist attitude whose essence is a tragic pose and learned metaphysical sneer'.[2]

Published in an expensive edition by Faber, and accompanied by an influential preface from T. S. Eliot, however, *Nightwood* demanded the full attention of the modernist literary scene, and was more typically acclaimed, in long reviews by important and reputable critics, as a masterpiece of modern fiction to be placed alongside the best work of Proust, Joyce and Eliot. The *Brooklyn Eagle* recommended it as 'an excellent companion piece for "The Waste Land" '; a reviewer in the *New Statesman and Nation* described it as 'a view of modern civilisation and contemporary social life that, for bitterness and crazy violence, leaves the darkest chapters of *Ulysses* far behind'; and the *New York Herald Tribune* compared Barnes's ability to spread a 'quality of moonlight over dissolution' with the work of Proust and Baudelaire, and the 'corrosive bluntness' of her tongue with Joyce.[3] The young Dylan Thomas argued that the novel could only be read as 'A Bible of Evil' by 'intellectual flippitygibbits', and that 'honest people who like beautiful writing' would recognize it as 'one of the three great prose books ever written by a woman'.[4]

If the original impulse for *Nightwood* was the agonizing loss of Thelma Wood, in the published novel Barnes paralleled a private love story with the broader cultural malaise of modernity, creating, through sordid scenes, grotesque characters and gallows humour, a vision of modern despair that is symbolic of all outcasts from an intolerant society. Analysing the social and psychological spaces of an urban modernity of the 'dispossessed', she presents a searing indictment of the construction and regulation of concepts of the orthodox and the taboo, at a time when sexual, racial and national difference was acquiring newly violent resonance.

WHAT OF THE NIGHT?

Nightwood begins with the death of an Austrian baroness, the birth of a Jew and the implied collapse of European imperialism. The Vienna of 1880 in which it opens was a city fraught with political and social tension, its large, assimilated Jewish establishment facing an increasingly virulent anti-Semitism. Hedvig Volkbein bears her child with 'a well-founded suspicion as to the advisability of perpetuating that race which has the sanction of the Lord and the disapproval of the people' (*N* 1), thrusting him from her before dying of the fever that has already taken her husband. Felix Volkbein is left an orphan, yet heir to the fake aristocratic title and genealogy fabricated by his father, an Italian Jew. Reintroduced in his 30s, Felix inherits his father's worship of nobility, and of the 'woman Austria' (*N* 42) of Habsburg myth, but also his inability to erase the racial memory of Jewishness, 'the step of the wandering Jew [that] is in every son' (N 7). He spends his life drifting around urban Europe in the company of a strange collection of theatre people, circus performers and social misfits. Attending a sickbed with the quack gynaecologist Dr Matthew O'Connor, Felix meets an American girl, Robin Vote. Collapsed in deep unconsciousness, Robin is introduced as a portrait for Felix and O'Connor's gaze, resembling a painting by Rousseau:

> On a bed, surrounded by a confusion of potted plants, exotic palms and cut flowers [. . .] half flung off the support of the cushions from which, in a moment of threatened consciousness she had turned her head, lay the young woman, heavy and dishevelled. Her legs, in white flannel trousers, were spread as in a dance, the thick lacquered pumps looking too lively for the arrested step. Her hands, long and beautiful, lay on either side of her face.
>
> The perfume that her body exhaled was of the quality of that earth-flesh, fungi, which smells of captured dampness and yet is so dry, overcast with the odour of oil of amber [. . .] Her flesh was the texture of plant life, and beneath it one sensed a frame, broad, porous and sleep-worn, as if sleep were a decay fishing her beneath the visible surface. (N 31)

The organic imagery of Robin's body contrasts with the lesbian chic of her Dietrich-style look, and her room, full of exotic plants and cut flowers, suggests 'a jungle trapped in a drawing room' (N 31). Barnes had been fascinated by images of animal/human morphology from her earliest work, and Robin embodies the vestiges of primitive animal spirit remaining embedded somewhere beneath the palimpsest of human memory. This state of 'beast turning human' (N 33), is one of pure abjection and liminality, a condition that is always at the point of metamorphosis between the animal and the human. Robin's pagan profanity also links her with the stereotypical image of the vampire. Described as 'the infected carrier of the past' and 'eaten death returning' (N 34), she resembles Pater's Madonna of the Rocks, her smile 'only in the mouth, and a little bitter: the face of an incurable yet to be stricken with its malady'. Felix cares only for the fact that she is American, however, idealizing her as the woman who might perpetuate his line with a son 'who would feel as he felt about the "great past" ' (N 35). Robin marries him and becomes pregnant, but restlessly takes to wandering across the cities of Europe, seeking escape from the confines of domesticity and her body in inebriation and promiscuity. She finally gives birth to a weak and mentally backward child, Guido, and leaves Felix soon afterwards. In an archetypal version of eugenicist degeneration theory, the mock 'House of Volkbein' will end in mental deformity; neither the vigorous blood of Felix's Austrian mother, nor that of his American wife, can dilute the taint of Jewishness.

The narrative breaks after Robin's disappearance and shifts to New York, where she meets the American heiress Nora Flood, a publicist for the circus and hostess of the 'strangest "salon" in America. [. . .] the "pauper's" salon, for poets, radicals, beggars, artists, and people in love; for Catholics, Protestants, Brahmins, dabblers in black magic and medicine' (N 45). Despite her affluent pose of bohemianism, however, Nora has in fact internalized the moral perspective of her American heritage, and she colludes with the very dictates of social order that she pretends to reject. Just as Felix is bound to the racial memory of his Jewishness, and Robin to the pull of a primitive past, Nora is 'known instantly as a Westerner' (N 45), her ancestry that of the Puritan founders of the New World, 'God so ponderous in their minds that they could stamp out the world with him in seven days' (N 46). Her lesbian desire for Robin is conducted entirely through a frame of monogamous domesticity. While she desperately wants to possess Robin, Nora's understanding of love and desire is ultimately conventional, her inversion merely a reflection of the heterosexual male.

Robin, by contrast, despite a conscious fear of her lack of identity and direction that leads her to require commitment from others, instinctively rejects confinement, and the force of Nora's love soon leads her again to frenzies of wantonness and alcoholism. When she leaves for another woman, Jenny Petheridge, Nora is distraught and turns imploringly to O'Connor to help her understand her loss. Their monologues dominate the rest of the book, in long sections describing fragmentary memories and dreams, in which most of the events of Robin and Nora's relationship are retrospectively conveyed, and the concept of the 'night' is explored.

The world of the night is the metonym by which Barnes expresses the repressive oppositional culture of modern society and its categorization of the normal and the perverse. For the modernist expatriate, repressive equated with American, and in the incompatibility of the worlds of 'night' and 'day', Barnes presents a Jamesian contrast between the profane, sensual and amoral culture of urban Europe and the puritanical, provincial and hypocritical paralysis of America. 'The night and the day are two travels', O'Connor tells Nora, but only the Frenchman, who does not deny his 'sediment, animal and vegetable' (N 76), accepts his journey through both. The American 'separates the two for fear of indignities' (N 76), and, '[tearing] up one for the sake of the other' (N 74), censors the mysteries of the night, and its associations with the instinctive and the carnal, in favour of the order of the day and the control of the rational mind. It is Western culture's need to consolidate its own stability that defines the abject as evil and debased. Perversity is defined by society when its conventions are transgressed, and whether designated as evil or pathological, the perceived need is always to police such violation. The result is an agony of self-denial and a frantic need to find meaning. Part of Nora's tragedy is that she has internalized the repressive sexual morality of her American puritan heritage and denigrates her desires, making Robin into a mirror on which she projects her own concern with the moral and the perverse. Yet Robin's dissipated peregrinations, O'Connor suggests, are attempts to recall an identity that evolution has failed to entirely bury:

> The French are dishevelled, and wise, the American tries to approximate it with drink. It is his only clue to himself. He takes it when his soap has washed him too clean for identification. The Anglo-Saxon has made the literal error; using water he has washed away his page. Misery melts him down by day, and sleep at night. His preoccupation with his business day has made his sleep insoluble. (N 80)

Robin exists within a pre-socialized conception of identity and behaviour, as if she has never grown from the infant as described by Freud, who begins life as inherently bisexual and polygamous, and who must renounce these perversions in order to become a socialized and gendered individual. The somnambulant, she exists between or beyond past and future, night and day, good and evil. As O'Connor comments, the sleeper is 'the proprietor of an unknown land. He goes about another business in the dark' (*N* 78). It is Nora, unable to follow Robin into the dreamworld of the night, who awakens her from her innocence and forces her into guilt and shame, by slapping her into consciousness. Robin responds by identifying more strongly with the perverse, but with a newly awakened knowledge of her immorality. As Nora finally recounts in horror, 'No rot had touched her until then, and there before my eyes I saw her corrupt all at once and withering, because I had struck her sleep away' (*N* 131).

DECADENT MODERNISM: JEWS, INVERTS AND THE ABJECT

Eliot's description of *Nightwood* as an aesthetic work of modernist experimentalism, the early focus of reviewers on its part decadent and part surreal imagery of dream and nightmare, and the principles of formalist criticism, led to a long tendency to overlook historical and social context in accounts of the novel. With the publication of Jane Marcus's ground-breaking essay, 'Laughing at Leviticus' (1991), however, interest in Barnes's engagement with the cultural and political conditions of her time increased.[5] '*Nightwood* is about merging, dissolution, and, above all, hybridization', states Marcus, arguing for a political project to the novel in which, by breaking the taboos of the Old Testament book of Leviticus and emphasizing disorder and aberrance from the norm, Barnes critiques a Western and increasingly fascist social order obsessed with the identification and regulation of the alien and the impure.

In 1931, during a trip to Munich with Ford when she was taking notes for *Nightwood*, Barnes had met Oswald Spengler, who discussed with her his theory of the inevitable decline of Western civilization.[6] A widespread fear of the collapse of a decadent and exhausted West at the end of the nineteenth century, caused by the destabilization of traditional notions of man's identity and supremacy by evolutionary science and growing secularization, had resulted in fresh attempts to construct and maintain a model of the autonomous bourgeois human subject. It is the modern anxiety about the instability of the body that pervades the themes, images, politics and metaphors of *Nightwood*.[7] Michel Foucault argues, for example, that at the end of the nineteenth century, as modern society increasingly became a culture of surveillance and self-regulation, a shift of concern took place from acts to identities, and, specifically, from the prohibition of deviant behaviour to the definition of deviant sexual and racial identities.[8] Man became:

> a personage, a past, a case history, and a childhood, in addition to being a type of life, a life form, and a morphology, with an indiscreet anatomy and possibly a mysterious physiology. Nothing that went into his total composition was unaffected by his sexuality. It was everywhere present in him: at the root of all his actions because it was their insidious and indefinitely active principle; written immodestly on his face and body because it was a secret that always gave itself away.[9]

'New' sciences of sociology, criminal anthropology, sexology and psychoanalysis, reconceptualized identity, producing definitions and hierarchical classifications of the human body and psyche, in order to pursue the self-contradictory project of affirming the 'normative' out of the definition of its opposite. From Nikka the bear-fighter's tattooed body to Matthew O'Connor's ribald commentary, bodies in *Nightwood* are sites of obscene inscription, as Barnes explores the production and regulation of normative models of sexual, cultural and racial identity, and their construction of the otherness of sexual, social and racial dissidence as deviant and taboo. In contrast to the white American, who has erased his body 'text', 'washed away his page' (*N* 80) with moral cleanliness, Nikka 'the nigger' (*N* 14) makes literal the mark of sexual or racial perversity that is written on the body, parading the discourses with which he has been constructed as 'other' through the painting of his flesh, 'tattooed from head to heel with all the *ameublement* of depravity' (*N* 14). Robin presents a blank slate, a body that mediates between the cultured and the primitive and is puzzling because it is therefore undefinable.

Nightwood presents the Church as the dominant force in creating the charged site of the corporeal body from the early modern period, but also implicates cultural anthropology, sexology and psychoanalysis in the West's construction of the ideal and obscene body, and the complex interaction between conceptions of sexuality, gender, race and the primitive. As Eliot states in a particularly discerning passage in his preface, psycho-theoretical narratives of perversity were not dissimilar from their religious predecessors:

> In the Puritan morality that I remember, it was tacitly assumed that if one was thrifty, enterprising, intelligent, practical and prudent in not violating social conventions, one ought to have a happy and 'successful' life. Failure was due to some weakness or perversity peculiar to the individual; but the decent man need have no nightmares. It is now rather more common to assume that all individual misery is the fault of 'society', and it is remediable by alterations from without. Fundamentally, the two philosophies, however different they may appear in operation, are the same.

Marcus argues, moreover, that *Nightwood* reveals a disturbing affinity between such discourses and the newly intolerant politics of 1930s Europe: 'Freud and fascism, by labeling deviance medically and politically, expose the inhumanity of the madness for order in every denial of difference from Leviticus to the sex doctors, Krafft-Ebbing, Havelock Ellis, Otto Weininger, and even Freud himself'.[10] Weininger's virulently anti-Semitic and misogynistic *Sex and Character* (1903), which defined polarized principles of masculinity (associated with the intellect, rationality and will) and femininity (the flesh, instinct and the amoral) emerging from an original bisexual state, was extremely popular and influential in literary and cultural circles, being translated into English in 1906 and still being reprinted in 1920. Its legacy is suggested in *Nightwood* by the atmosphere of cultural degeneration, and Barnes's representation of the interconnection of Jew, woman and sexual deviant as abject figures in a pure and vigorous society. Barnes's critique of the sexologists and of Freud, however, is perhaps more complicated; involving at once a rejection of the patriarchal authority of the male medical mind over the transgressive body, and an awareness of their contribution to sexual liberation and women's rights.

In Radclyffe Hall's *The Well of Loneliness*, the heroine Stephen Gordon learns of her aberrant sexual identity when she finds a book, covered with annotations, in her father's library: 'Krafft-Ebing – she had never heard of the author before. [. . .] She began to read, sitting down rather abruptly'.[11] Richard von Krafft-Ebing's *Psychopathia Sexualis* (1886; translated into English in 1892) reconceptualized sexuality by drawing a distinction between sexual 'perversion', a congenital and thus involuntary condition of abnormal sexual development, and sexual 'perversity', a vice and moral weakness: 'The determining factor here is the demonstration of perverse feeling for the same sex; not the proof of sexual acts with the same sex. These two phenomena must not be confounded with each other; perversity must not be taken for perversion'.[12] Hall's novel, drawing on this distinction for its defence of lesbianism, was published in 1928, accompanied by an introduction by another eminent sexologist, Havelock Ellis, who agreed with Krafft-Ebing on the congenital nature of what they called 'inversion'. Ellis's *Sexual Inversion* (1897), the first of his multi-volume *Studies in the Psychology of Sex* (1897–1928) was perhaps the most influential study of deviant sexual behaviour at the end of the nineteenth century. It was banned for obscenity in 1898, forcing Ellis to publish the rest of his work from America, gaining a large professional and popular readership.

The intellectual consciousness of Barnes's Greenwich Village milieu in the 1910s and 1920s was extremely receptive to the new social-scientific and psycho-medical discourses, principally to the work of Freud, which was widely translated and popularized. It is important, however, to recognize the enduring influence of sexology at the time.[13] Barnes's writing indicates that she was well versed in Freudian concepts, and notably the understanding of sexuality as rooted in the struggle between the desires of the unconscious and the demands of modern civilization, but there is little evidence that she approached psychoanalysis with anything other than ambivalence, regarding it as just one of a history of reductive disciplinary systems of identity. The regular use of the words 'invert' or 'inversion' in *Nightwood*, however, along with the numerous figures of blurred gender identity (the androgyne, hermaphrodite, transvestite and invert) that occur frequently throughout her works, suggests a sustained interest in the possibilities of transgender identity. Sexology can without doubt be accused of pathologizing inversion and working within rigid heterosexual paradigms, in which homosexuality could only be understood in terms of the 'womanly man' or 'manly woman'. On the other hand, the numerous labels it was forced to produce for the broad and complex range of cross-gender behaviours discovered in its case studies do to a certain degree explode the project of reductive classification itself.

If inversion was a principal subject of the new sciences of sexology and psychoanalysis at the turn of the century, it was also an increasingly visual spectacle within the public spaces of Europe's cities, Proust writing in *Sodom and Gomorrah* of the numerous descendants of Sodom, the first city of sin, who now inhabited London, Paris, Berlin and Rome. As in *Nightwood*, the comedy theatre of Paris and Berlin in the 1920s and 1930s was associated with an urban demi-monde and homosexual subculture. During the Carnival celebrations of Lent in Paris, revived in the 1920s, when the law against transvestism was relaxed, thousands of men in extravagant female dress attended annual masked balls at 'Magic-City', a dance-hall near the Eiffel Tower.[14] Berlin, which attracted expatriate Americans from Paris because of its desperate economy and massive inflation, was even more renowned as a centre of transgressive sexuality, however, and where Magnus Hirschfeld set up his Institute for the Study of Sexual Sciences in 1919.

In *Die Transvestiten* (1910), Hirschfeld had argued for the existence of a diverse range of transgender identities and practices, his case studies producing such an accumulation of categories that by the end, 'all subjects [were] revealed in some sense as transgendered: there is no absolute man or woman, but only degrees of sex and gender crossing'.[15] Transgender identities, with their quality of hybridity, impurity and cross-breeding, fit appropriately with Barnes's broader depiction of the liminality and disordered bodies of Europe's social outcasts, and when Barnes was in Berlin with Thelma Wood,

Berenice Abbott, Robert McAlmon and Marsden Hartley in 1921, they rented rooms near the Institute on the In den Zelten. McAlmon later described in his memoirs that 'Hirschfeld was conducting his psychoanalytic school and a number of souls unsure of their sexes or of their inhibitions competed with each other in looking or acting freakishly', continuing, 'At nights along the Unter den Linden it was never possible to know if it was a woman or a man in woman's clothes who accosted one'.[16] Berlin was a city in which 'there was no gaiety or joy, only recklessness, wildness'.[17] McAlmon recalled that Barnes rarely visited the all-night clubs as she was working and 'did not, as did most of the others, do night life', but she drew on its milieu for the limbo-like environment of *Nightwood*, merging both Paris and Berlin into the fluid space of an itinerant and liminal subculture.[18]

Sexology's theory of 'inversion', along with the discourse and vocabulary that elaborated it, contributed to what Jeffrey Weeks has described as 'a homosexual self-consciousness' enabling inverts to voice their own identity, even if only through the same terms as those with which they were identified.[19] Although Barnes employs the disqualifying vocabulary of the new sciences in *Nightwood*, any presentation of a reverse discourse is at best ambivalent, however, an aspect of the novel that many critics find troubling or ignore. Bonnie Kime Scott, for example, notes that *Nightwood* depicts an intermediate space between the dualities of body and mind, beast and saint, nature and culture, instinct and intellect that order social identity; she argues that Barnes 'encourages us to see this territory as a place of discovery'.[20] Yet what is revealed by or learned within this space is ultimately a bitter knowledge of its own liminality. *Nightwood* alerts the reader to the repressive construction of concepts of marginality and deviancy, and challenges the social, sexual and religious discourses that have claimed authority for their pathologization, yet the murky territory of the 'night' remains institutionally structured and defined in terms of the binary order as a limbo for the unassimilable. This is not to suggest that Barnes advocates the perspective of the 'normal', but that she recognizes the limits of an ahistoricized carnivalesque reversal as an aesthetic and political strategy. As Diane

Chisholm has astutely argued, 'Barnes strongly resists the tendency that animated her amazonian contemporaries to elaborate and glorify "inversion"; instead, she flaunts a queer scepticism concerning sexual liberation and its bohemian milieux'.[21]

Joseph Allen Boone, in *Libidinal Currents: Sexuality and the Shaping of Modernism*, also draws on contemporary queer theory to overcome the restrictions of a 'lesbian' or 'feminist' fiction agenda, and to explore the complexities and ambiguities of what he calls Barnes's 'perverse aesthetics' through a fluidity or polymorphism of, specifically, sexual identities and spaces, but also, more broadly, all behaviours categorized as non-normative, different and thus deviant.[22] Boone suggests that Barnes foregrounds an underworld of 'outcasts' who 'revel in their outlaw and pariah status, embracing their supposed "damnation" and parading their abjection as a sign of divine election'. This assumes an alternative discourse of the marginalized similar to that of Kime Scott (and one, moreover, that is difficult to substantiate from the misery and torment that is suffered without relent by the characters in the text). However, Boone does provide an illuminating context for the deliberate waywardness of Barnes's sexual/textual aesthetics when he argues that, 'in mapping the instability and variability of psychosexual impulses and in tracking the dispersive, wayward trajectories that the libido etches in the subconscious, [. . .] modern fictions of sexuality have produced [. . .] a poetics and politics of the perverse'.[23] Thematic depiction of the perverse, which is validated as the condition of pre-Oedipal sexuality, extends into a use of language and experimentation with style and form that is also polymorphous, a social, sexual, structural and linguistic rejection of the 'normal' dualistic or binary order. It is this 'poetics of the perverse', elaborated through the energy of the Rabelaisian bawdy and the profane mysticism of surrealism, that transforms *Nightwood* from a work of decadence to one of modernism. Through a deliberately deviant aesthetic, dealing thematically with violence, hedonism, abnormality and self-denial, and stylistically with extravagance, rhetoric and epigrammatic posturing, Barnes charts a new space of representation.

WHAT OF THE NIGHT? AN AESTHETICS OF
PERVERSITY

Nightwood's urban phantasmagoria, with its cast of ragpickers, hysterics and *femmes damnées,* is part of a tradition of subjective topography that extends from Victor Hugo and Charles Baudelaire to Marcel Proust and the surrealism of André Breton and Walter Benjamin. Paris, for these writers, is at once the city of modernity, the 'capital of the nineteenth century', and the city in which the past, on the point of collapse, holds tenaciously to the spatial enclaves it has sequestered. Its landscape is socially, psychologically and geographically perverse, a palimpsest of the debased spaces, texts and histories of urban Europe. '[T]hose who love a city, in its profoundest sense, become the shame of that city, the détraqués, the paupers' (*N* 47), Barnes writes towards the beginning of the novel, and Nora Flood later comments that 'the pauper is the rudiment of a city, knowing something of the city, which the city, for its own destiny, wants to forget' (*N* 141). The double aspect of the city suggested by Barnes resembles Michel de Certeau's differentiation of the rational, 'concept' city envisioned by the urban planner and the 'primitive' city of withdrawn memories and fantasies. The existence of the *espace propre* of the former, states de Certeau, depends on its ability to 'repress all the physical, mental and political pollutions that would compromise it' into an urban unconscious of illegitimate spatial practices. 'Beneath the discourses that ideologize the city, the ruses and combinations of powers that have no readable identity proliferate: without points where one can take hold of them, without rational transparency, they are impossible to administer'.[24] It is this underworld that, in *Nightwood*, becomes a repository for those whom society designates as abject and obscene; Jews, neurotics, physical freaks and sexual inverts.

Most of *Nightwood* is set against the low-culture entertainment sites of Berlin and the Parisian Left Bank; the circus, comedy theatre and carnival, spaces of 'splendid and reeking falsification' (*N* 10), to which Felix, Nora Flood and O'Connor all turn. Comedy theatre, based in the tradition of the commedia-dell'arte, was hugely popular in metropolitan culture from the late nineteenth century to the 1930s. As a lowbrow, illegitimate art form which revels in its vulgarity and parades its artifice, the comedy theatre fascinated the European modernist avant-garde. Barnes adored its milieu and was a regular visitor, along with the photographer Berenice Abbott, whom Barnes had known in Greenwich Village and through whom she met Thelma Wood in 1921. With its transvestism, masks and social satire, the circus upturned categories of reality and performance, wisdom and foolery, beauty and abjection, culture and bestiality. Such carnivalesque, however, can only ever achieve the brief subversive power of sanctioned deviance, parodying or providing a contrast to the hierarchies, binarisms and disciplines of a dominant social order, yet at the same time ultimately replicating and reinforcing them. Barnes, as in her earlier journalism, recognizes that the comedy theatre itself is a site of estrangement and oppression for its performers. The absurdist laughter and mask of satiric humour with which it presents itself, however, suggests a 'perverse aesthetics' similar to Barnes's own. The ambiguity with which she presents the urban underworld, I argue, is thus the result of her refusal to reduce the subtleties of this illegitimate space to the sort of 'readable identity' that, as de Certeau observes, its very existence makes impossible.

More illuminating is to consider this space and its denizens in terms of Julia Kristeva's formulation of 'abjection' in *Powers of Horror*, in which she interprets the abject as a state of ambiguous and therefore transgressive identity, the human subject who aspires or pretends to individual selfhood yet is ultimately a spectacle of its breakdown. The circus performers, for example, assume aristocratic distinction with their grand sobriquets of Princess Nadja, Baron von Tink, the Principessa Stasera y Stasero, King Buffo and the Duchess of Broadback, yet are 'gaudy, cheap cuts from the beast life' (*N* 10), figures who are not fully human and merge in bizarre forms with animal or machine. What is crucial to Kristeva's analysis, however, is the ambiguity not only of morphic identity but also of the experience *of being* 'abject'; consisting of both the positive embrace of abjection that leads to *jouissance*, or an anxiety of difference and alienation. O'Connor and the circus troupe may exuberantly display their physical distortions, but Volkbein

73

and Nora Flood, in contrast, turn all the more fanatically to conventionally sanctioned identities.

Doctor Matthew O'Connor, back-street abortionist and closet transvestite with a desire for young boys, is the self-acclaimed guide to the Circean 'nightworld' and the *flâneur* of its urban habitat. O'Connor is a fictional portrait of Daniel Mahoney, a bawdy medical quack and boastful homosexual, prominent in numerous memoirs of the period and whom Barnes knew well as a friend and drinking partner.[25] The Canadian writer John Glassco described him in *Memoirs of Montparnasse* as 'Dr Maloney', whose self-aggrandizing conversation revolved around 'unmentionable subjects and indescribable practices', yet who was also 'the most-quoted homosexual in Paris, a man who combined the professions of pathic, abortionist, professional boxer and quasi-confessor to literary women'.[26] Phillip Herring notes that Barnes would take copious notes while he talked, and Charles Henri Ford wrote, 'D . . . calls him her *copy* and does turn his lines remembered from 20 years back into brilliant prose'.[27] Barnes's friendship with Mahoney was tempestuous, the latter both proud of and insulted by his portrayal in *Nightwood*, but they remained in contact until his death in 1959. He provided for Barnes a prism of the past, and she stated in a letter just before his death that, 'writing to you is like that Proustian *madeleine* – and that uneven courtyard stone that sent him pitching headfirst into his past', continuing, 'I hope that you are not too somber, that you have some of your former hilarious sorrow'.[28]

The narrow and winding streets of the Paris Latin quarter present a stark contrast to the modern open boulevards of Haussman's Right Bank, and seem to carry the weight of history, the 'odour of memory' (*N* 107) in which Robin senses her identity. Like Robin, O'Connor haunts the ancient churches and hunts the homosexual cruising grounds of the Place St Sulpice and Place de la Bastille, constructing the geography of the night out of both the sacred and the profane. O'Connor's principal role, as Carroll Smith-Rosenberg has perceptively noted, is to act as a 'trickster' character, a modern version of the Renaissance fool who 'specifically embodies the disorder and the creative power we associate with liminality, a creature who exists to break taboos, violate categories, and defy structure'. His narratives attack and reverse social order, and are vigorously expressed in the bawdy style of the Restoration, when promiscuity and extravagance were celebrated as a social norm with which to replace years of restraint by the Puritan ethic. His speech is vivid and blazoning, his phrasing witty and his language robust, but his epigrammatic narratives are dark parables of sin and damnation, the madness of a clown who mixes absurd humour and nihilistic despair.

Turning again to Burton's *Anatomy of Melancholy*, and its satiric paraphrasing of medical and philosophical theory, Barnes makes O'Connor a profane alchemist, his schizophrenic pronouncements combining the rhetoric of the priest, gynaecologist, sexologist and psychoanalyst in a conflation of obscene confession and talking cure, as well as the dadaist protesting against the sacred and rational systems of society with vociferous obscenity. Felix is surprised to find that the flowers laid at the church altars 'were placed there by the people of the underworld' and that the reddest is 'the rose of the doctor' (*N* 28), but O'Connor reveres the erotic mysticism of the Church at the same time as he pours blasphemy on its authoritative institutionalism. His is an American modernist sensibility that recognizes religion as the repressive white, liberalist and middle-class orthodoxy of the Puritan Church on which it was reared, and which it vehemently rejected, and yet found in European Catholicism an exotic occultism. For O'Connor, the Catholic Church 'is the girl that you love so much that she can lie to you' (*N* 18), and who pretends the forgiveness of sin through the confessional, where 'in sonorous prose, lacking contrition (if you must) you can speak of the condition of the knotty, tangled soul and be answered in Gothic echoes, mutual and instantaneous – one saying hail to your farewell' (*N* 19). The modern Protestant Church, by contrast, offers only the 'obscene megalomania' (*N* 18) of Christian rhetoric, encouraging denial and self-deception, rather than confession and self-awareness.

In the world of modernity, when religion has become little more than a discourse of moral regulation, supporting a host of other such discourses, the ritualism of Catholicism can provide a degree of relief. Robin too turns to Catholicism when she is pregnant with Guido, taking its vows and visiting many churches to pray. Like the sufferers of Dante's limbo, however, her heathen soul cannot find salvation because it does not understand the notion of either sin or absolution: 'her prayer was monstrous, because in it there was no margin left for damnation or forgiveness, for praise or for blame – those who cannot conceive a bargain cannot be saved or damned' (*N* 42).

As one reviewer noted, the chapter title 'Go Down, Matthew' refers to 'at once a homosexual joke, a call to prayer and a command to descend into Inferno'.[29] O'Connor describes himself as a born invert, a woman trapped within a male body:

> Am I to blame if I've been summoned before and this is my last and oddest call? In the old days I was possibly a girl in Marseilles thumping the dock with a sailor, and perhaps it's the memory that haunts me. The wise men say that the remembrance of things past is all that we have for a future, and am I to blame if I've turned up this time as I shouldn't have been, when it was a high soprano I wanted, and deep corn curls to my bum, with a womb as big as the king's kettle and a bosom as high as the bowspit of a fishing schooner?' (*N* 81)

He approximates his fantasies through cross-dressing. When Nora Flood intrudes on the doctor at home, for example, at the beginning of the chapter 'Watchman, What of the Night?', she finds him in bed, 'heavily rouged and his lashes painted', wearing a woman's night-gown and 'the golden semi-circle of a wig with long pendant curls that touched his shoulders', a scene reminiscent of the Circe section of *Ulysses* in which Leopold Bloom is transformed into a mincing, petticoated woman, and a grotesque parody of the fake adornments of womanhood. His room is at once both boudoir and abortion chamber, the instruments of his female guise mingling with those of his profession: 'a rusty pair of forceps, a broken scalpel, half a dozen odd instruments that she could not place, a catheter, some twenty perfume bottles, almost empty, pomades, creams, rouges, powder boxes and puffs'.

Inverting social values, O'Connor's cross-dressing effectively exposes the artificiality of the gender codes of construction of femininity as painful and unnatural. There is no suggestion that O'Connor might pass as a woman, however. His cross-dressing results not in successful transvestism, in which the male appears as a woman, but in the image of a man dressed in woman's garb that flaunts the illicitness of its act. Nora's immediate response is the recognition that, 'God, children know something they can't tell; they like Red Riding Hood and the wolf in bed' (*N* 71), an acknowledgement of childhood incestual desire that surfaces earlier in Nora's dream of her grandmother, 'dressed as a man, wearing a billycock and a corked moustache, ridiculous and plump in tight trousers and a red waistcoat, her arms spread saying with a leer of love, "My little sweetheart!" ' (*N* 57), and later in her description of Robin as 'incest too' (*N* 141). In a surreal set of associations, O'Connor's role metamorphoses again, as he becomes one with both Robin and the grandmother, whose ringmaster outfit mimics his role as the novel's maestro, and a matriarchal authority for Nora herself.

Eliot regarded O'Connor as the most important character within the book, who makes of the novel 'a whole pattern' (*N* xi), an assessment that encourages the association of the doctor with Eliot's own Tiresias, the 'old man with wrinkled dugs' of *The Waste Land*. Like Tiresias, O'Connor is a perverse seer, who 'knows everything [. . .] because he's been everywhere at the wrong time and has now become anonymous' (*N* 74), and describes himself as 'a fisher of men' (*N* 87). Yet is Barnes's reference to the Fisher King of Eliot's poem a gesture of tribute or of ironic comparison? *Nightwood* ultimately refuses aesthetic order through its own perversity, undermining the authority of O'Connor, on whose diagnosis of the 'night' and its inhabitants the reader comes to depend. He provides the narrative of self-recrimination that articulates the suffering of the novel's culturally dispossessed, but denies it meaning, admitting, 'I am my own charlatan'.

'TOM, DARLING': ELIOT, EDITORSHIP AND OBSCENITY

Nightwood was written in the aftermath of Barnes's break with Thelma Wood in 1929, and the ardour and torment of their ten-year relationship forms the autobiographical context to the novel. A letter, written by Barnes to Emily Coleman in 1935, indicates that she began writing the novel, provisionally titled 'Bow Down', between 1931 and 1933, when she was struggling with Thelma's attempts at reconciliation, and amidst an affair with Ford: 'I wrote it you must remember [. . .] when I did not know whether Thelma would come back to me or not [. . .] whether I could live with her again or not; in that turmoil of Charles and Morocco, sickness, Hayford Hall – everything, then the end here in New York. [. . .] when I realised that being here was death (and is) for me'.[30] By April 1933 Barnes was with Ford in Tangier, revising an early typescript and worrying about his criticism of its lack of plot and design. In June she returned to Paris for an abortion, and then for convalescence to Hayford Hall, the Devon estate rented by Peggy Guggenheim where she had spent the previous summer, and where she read the draft novel aloud to Emily Coleman and Guggenheim's lover John Holms, making revisions in response to their criticisms. Sending this early version, under the original title of 'Bow Down', to T. R. Smith at Boni & Liveright, who had published *Ryder*, Barnes received a reply advising substantial revision:

> The early part of the book is clear enough but it soon becomes obscured in nothing more than a welter of homosexuality, described and analyzed. It is obvious to me that you have tried to do an honest study of perversion but I am afraid you got lost in your studies. There is so much brilliant writing, so much unusually broad observation of life and behavior, so much keen philosophy, that it is a pity that the book succeeds only in being a rambling, obscure complicated account of what the average reader will consider 'God knows what'.[31]

Having been rejected by reportedly 'every publisher' in America, the manuscript was finally accepted for publication by T. S. Eliot and Frank Morley at Faber in 1936, after substantial alteration by Barnes under the advice of Emily Coleman, who cajoled Eliot into reading it. Eliot was impressed with the novel, writing to Geoffrey Faber, 'I believe this may be our last chance to do something remarkable in the way of imaginative literature'.[32] Publication remained dependent, however, on Barnes's amenability to 'small omissions' of material which Eliot feared would incite the censor. The extent of his further influence has been a concern for the majority of Barnes scholars, described as controlling by Jane Marcus, 'posturing' by Phillip Herring and, more sympathetically, as 'well-meant management' by Tyrus Miller.[33] Although critics have tended to accuse Eliot of treating the text harshly, however, as the canonical modernist dictator diluting the subversive abjection of the woman writer's text, the publication of the original text and drafts reveals that his alterations were relatively minor. Whilst the only editor prepared to accept the troubling themes and narrative style of the book, Eliot nevertheless blurred the more overt descriptions of sexual perversion and of religious profanity, as well as moderating obscene language.

The main passages to receive modification were predictably O'Connor's monologues, the alterations usually directed at explicitly homosexual or blasphemous references. His description of the female sodomites of the night, for example, which Emily Coleman described as the ' "damnation in the toilet" passage' and 'the most awful in the book', underwent substantial revision. In the published text, O'Connor tells Nora of the girls who 'turn day into night' (*N* 84), existing in a limbo in which they cry for physical annihilation as they '[lie] upon the floor, face down, with that terrible longing of the body that would, in misery, be flat with the floor; lost lower than burial, utterly blotted out and erased so that no stain of her could ache upon the wood' (*N* 85). The sodomite desires to extinguish herself and blot out the stain that is the mark of her body. He continues:

> Look for the girls also in the toilets at night, and you will find them kneeling in that great secret confessional, crying between tongues, the terrible excommunication: 'May you be damned to hell! May you die standing upright! May you be damned upward! May this be damned, terrible and damned spot! May it wither into the grin of the dead, may this draw back, low riding mouth in an empty snarl of the groin! May this be your torment, may this be your damnation! God damned me before you, and after me you shall be damned, kneeling and standing away till we vanish! [. . .] May you pass from me, damned girl! Damned and betraying!' 'There's a curse for you,' he said, 'and I have heard it.' (*N* 85)

The early manuscript presents a more explicit blasphemy and depiction of lesbianism, reading: 'that great second confessional, the one the Catholic church forgot – over the door Dames, a girl standing before her, her skirts flung back one on one, while between the columns of the handsome head of the girl made boy by God, bends back, the posture of that head volts forth the difference between one woman and another that great second confessional' (N 262).[34] The women suffer from a masochistic internalization of their perversity as both sexual women and lesbians, damning their sexuality and wretchedly repudiating desires that they cannot deny. The concern to erase the stigmata of deviancy, as with Felix and his father's attempts to hide their Jewishness, again disturbingly predicts Hitler's projects for racial and social purity. The 'damned and terrible spot', which in the expurgated passage reads as the spot of menstrual blood, with the further reference implies the spot or place of female sexual pleasure, the clitoris. Eliot, alert to the threat of censorship, prompted the prudent obscuring of the passage, yet in general, given the obvious lesbian plot, extensive ribald language and blatant discussion of homosexuality that remain in the published novel, his editorial pen seems to have been at once mild and rather arbitrary.

Perhaps the most significant change that Eliot advised and that Barnes *resisted* was the substitution of the word 'unclean' for 'obscene' in the final episode of the novel, in which Nora follows her dog to the chapel on her estate, where she finds Robin crawling on all fours with him before the altar. It is the passage that has aroused most critical controversy over possible obscenity, with both current critics and Barnes's contemporaries reading the passage as a reference to bestial sexuality. In a letter to Barnes in 1935, for example, Emily Coleman states of the manuscript, 'you actually have made this dog sexual. But it can be made less so. It isn't that publishers wouldn't like it – it is that you do not want that idea there yourself'. On the typescript with Eliot's corrections the scene reads:

> Sliding down she went; down, her hair swinging, her arms held out, and the dog stood there, rearing back, his forelegs slanting; his paws trembling under the trembling of his rump, his hackle standing; his mouth open, his tongue slung sideways over his sharp bright teeth; whining and waiting. And down she went, until her head swung against his; on all fours now, dragging her knees. (N 152)

It continues, 'Then she began to bark also, crawling after him – barking in a fit of laughter, obscene and touching' (*N* 153). Eliot crosses out 'obscene' here and writes 'unclean' in the margin. Barnes's handwriting then adds, 'Sample of T.S.E.'s "lack of imagination" '. The published passage, unrevised, excited discussion, and the cultural message of the passage was largely taken to be a perverse one, reviewers drawing on the connotations of the phrase 'to go down'. Barnes herself, however, denied any sexual significance to Robin's act, arguing that it was the culmination of the girl's desperate instinctive attempt to cling to her animal origins and counter the process of 'turning human'. Chester Page, a close friend of Barnes in her later years, recalled in a letter to the *New York Times*, 'Miss Barnes resented the implications that the last pages of "Nightwood" represent bestiality. I remember her fury when some critic ventured that theory. She stated that the dog was simply terrorized by the sight of its mistress behaving in an irrational manner, and only that'.[35] Despite Barnes's denials, the question of whether Robin's act is or is not intentionally obscene is not really the most significant aspect of the scene. Indeed the act of 'going down', before the dog and before the altar of a Protestant chapel, is at once, as Chisholm recognizes, 'paradoxically sacred *and* profane'.[36]

It was probably the stylistic modernist abstraction of *Nightwood*, rather than the explicit details of Eliot's editing, that ultimately protected *Nightwood* from censorship. The basis for defining obscenity at this time was still the nineteenth-century Hicklin rule that judged 'whether the tendency of the matter charged as obscenity is to deprave and corrupt those whose minds are open to such immoral influences and into whose hands a publication of this sort may fall'.[37] It was on such grounds that Hall's *The Well of Loneliness* had been suppressed, after a sensationalist editorial by James Douglas in the *Sunday Express* ranted of the presentation of the invert protagonist, 'this pestilence is devastating the younger generation. It is wrecking young lives. It is defiling young souls'.

Far from attempting to explain and justify sexual inversion as a natural state, however, as Hall purposefully set out to do with *The Well of Loneliness*, *Nightwood* neither clearly supported nor condemned it, seeming to emphasize all sexual bodies as grotesque and to depict the experience of the invert and homosexual as one of suffering and horror. The reviewer for the *New Statesman and Nation*, for example, noting that 'The test of a book's obscenity is said to be its power of corrupting those who are open to corruption', stated that 'had I a daughter whose passions for mistresses and older girls were beginning to cause scandal and alarm, I should certainly insist that she read *Night Wood*'. Any further doubt would have been swayed by the authority of Eliot as editor, whose preface unsurprisingly became the convex lens through which most readers approached the novel. Seemingly anticipating obscenity charges, as his firm warning 'to anyone reading the book for the first time [. . .] the book is not a psychopathic study' (*N* xii) implies, Eliot directed the reader away from the specific connotations of sexual and psychological pathologies, towards an understanding of the novel that was firmly located within the context of a familiar modernist narrative; a vision of a fragmented, tormented humanity connected by an underlying unity, voiced, in this case, by the Tiresian figure of O'Connor:

> The book is not simply a collection of individual portraits; the characters are all knotted together, as people are in real life [. . .] it is the whole pattern that they form, rather than any individual constituent, that is the focus of interest. [. . .] the deeper design is that of the human misery and bondage which is universal. (*N* xii–xiii)

However, although the novel, with its fragmented form, tone of impotency and despair, and allusions to the Bible, Dante, Shakespeare, Webster, Swinburne and Baudelaire, seems fundamentally high modernist, Barnes ultimately seems to reject the ordering 'mythical method' advocated by Eliot the critic, turning instead to the confusion and dark liminality presented by Eliot the poet, himself the writer of 'one of the most abject texts in English literature'.[38] Barnes's allusions to primitive ritual, classical myth and Catholicism operate to different effect than high modernism's mythic quest for a holy grail of spiritual meaning. As Tyrus Miller astutely argues, *Nightwood* presents not the typically high modernist concern with the confusion of the individual trying to make sense of a bewildering cosmos, but rather the ontological uncertainty and complete 'progressive breakdown of character, the disintegration of the indices of "self" in fiction'.[39] O'Connor's speeches promise a message or explanation for the chaos and despair of the novel, yet he delivers the riddles of a madman who attempts to cheat anguish through 'hilarious sorrow', a vision of life perhaps at once more pessimistic and more stoical than that of Barnes's modernist contemporaries.

5

Epilogue: *The Antiphon*

On reading Joyce's *Ulysses* in 1922, Barnes remarked, 'I shall never write another line. Who has the nerve to after this?'[1] She went on to write *Ryder, Ladies Almanack* and *Nightwood*. Between *Nightwood* and her final major publication in 1958, the verse play *The Antiphon*, however, she published only one article. During this time she suffered a breakdown, retreated into alcoholism and was forced by both her ill health and her financial insolvency to return to New York. The article was significantly titled 'Lament for the Left Bank'.[2] In a letter to Emily Coleman in December 1937, she wrote, 'I begin to believe that *Nightwood* was written under a Svengali, that it is my only book, and there wont be any more', and ten months later, 'a woman's accident work of art is a whip behind her beating her out'.[3] After *Nightwood*, lacking confidence in her own ability to judge her work, she increasingly viewed Eliot as her Svengali. Unlike the inspiration provided by Joyce, however, her detachment from the environment of modernist experimentalism that had been Paris, and her dependence on Eliot's approval coupled with her desire to keep him as her editor appears to have obstructed her productivity.

Barnes began writing *The Antiphon*, which like *Ryder* presents a fictionalized account of her early family life, in the late 1940s, sending the manuscript to Eliot for Faber & Faber in 1954. His response was cautious but he passed it to Edwin Muir to act as reader. Muir, who responded well to Barnes's work, was predictably enthusiastic, although he recommended numerous cuts in the first act. Eliot finally accepted a revised version in 1956, still demanding further changes, and after numerous rewrites *The Antiphon* appeared in 1958, three hundred lines having been cut from earlier drafts.[4] When Barnes saw the preface that Eliot had written to accompany the text, however, she finally rebelled against his authority in exasperation. 'From the point of view of the conventionally minded', he wrote, employing the same strategy of detachment that he had used for *Nightwood*, 'THE ANTIPHON will be still more shocking – or would be if they could understand it – and still more tedious – because they will not understand it – than NIGHTWOOD', going on to say of Barnes, 'never has so much genius been combined with so little talent'.[5] Barnes regarded Eliot as a mentor and close friend, and was understandably hurt by this strangely mean commentary, with which Eliot could hardly have expected to aid sales. She immediately complained, with justification, of its negative effect, writing, 'I cannot recall seeing a "blurb" – which I had always thought a means of promoting a book – so tailored to a jacket that so resembles a shroud'.[6] In clipped reply Eliot withdrew his remarks, replacing them with a brief introduction of the play as 'the nearest thing written in our time to the grimmer and grislier tragedies of the Jacobean poets' and a more favourable comment from Edwin Muir that stated, 'THE ANTIPHON is one of the greatest things that have been written in our time, and it would be a disaster if it were never to be known'.[7]

The play is set in 1939 in Burley Hall, a ruined ancestral home in England, to which the surviving members of the Burley family have come together in an attempt to understand and mend the fissures caused by events in the past. Barnes had visited her mother's family home in Oakham, Leicestershire, in 1936, a trip which seems to have influenced the setting of the play. In a self-reflexive metaphor for the project of recollection that Barnes pursues in both *Ryder* and *The Antiphon*, the eldest son Jeremy, for some reason travelling in disguise as 'Jack Blow', has constructed a miniature replica of the farmhouse where they lived in America and which he calls 'Hobb's Ark, beast-box, doll's house' (*A* 181), placing in it small dolls that correspond to the family members; his father Titus and mother Augusta, his grandmother Victoria, and Miranda, Elisha and Dudley, his sister and conniving brothers. The current owner of Burley Hall, their uncle Jonathan, is also present. Titus and Victoria, the instigators of the family's torment, are now both

85

dead, but their figurines remain as reminders of both their ultimately mortal frailty and their nevertheless persistent influence on the present. The boys mock Titus irreverently as the 'old ram' and 'cock-pit bully boy' (*A* 151), and Augusta looks at his likeness from the detachment of the years, saying,

> How do we thaw from history? How many
> To this splinter have, like porcupines,
> Made careful love? What apes our eyes were
> Saw him great because he said so.

(A 183)

The text itself belies her words, however, for it emphasizes the continued strength of the past on the events and emotions of the present.

During the years that have passed, Miranda has achieved brief success as a writer in Paris, but is now escaping the city on the onset of war. Military occupation is thus also associated with the plunder and destruction of spaces associated with art and culture. Jeremy for example states:

> I expect to see myopic conquerors
> With pebbled monocles and rowel'd heels,
> In a damned and horrid clutch of gluttony
> Dredging the Seine of our inheritance.
> Or dragging from the Tiber and the Thames
> Cruppers, bridles, bits and casket handles;
> Rocking-horses and sabres from the fair.
> Trawling the Hellespont for log and legend
> And all things whatsoever out of grasp.

(A 91)

The cultural history of Europe, both classic (the Hellespont) and personal (the antiques from the fair that recall those collected by Barnes and Thelma Wood for their Paris apartment), has been seized by the clutch of war, as the threat of fascism that forms part of the brooding background of *Nightwood* becomes a reality. It was a connection that Barnes herself felt strongly. The war forced her to leave Paris, the city that she felt was crucial to her ability to write and where she determinedly remained until the last possible moment in October 1939. In March 1940, hating New York and its commercial values, quarrelling with her mother and succumbing to increasing alcoholism, she was committed to a sanatorium on Lake George by her brothers Saxon and Zendon. Writing to Emily Coleman at the time, Barnes describes the horrors and corruption of the asylum, 'where my family has put me by force'.[8] In another letter, she wrote that her brothers were interested only in 'money, money, money', and, complaining that her doctors were advising her to give up writing for a more stable and financially secure occupation, states 'I've got to forget or I starve; I've got to forget all my twenty years of Europe'.[9] A similar attack is made on Miranda's writing and unconventionality in *The Antiphon*, when Dudley blusteringly exclaims against her strange theatrical costume; 'A strolling player indeed! Without Protector,/ Husband, son, or bank-account? Phizz, phizz!' (*A* 168). Miranda herself at one point states, 'I fear brothers' (*A* 90). In an association of war and patriarchy, Barnes maps her memories of military and male domination onto one another in *The Antiphon*, paralleling the fighting in Europe and the degeneration of European civiliza-tion with the emotional battles of the family and their crumbling mansion.

Act I presents the basic history of the family through the discussions of Miranda, her brothers and their uncle. Family abuse and incest are the main themes of the play, and the reader is told again of events familiar from *Ryder*; the life of Titus and his mother in London, Titus's seduction of Augusta and Victoria's appropriation of her inheritance, his constant polygamy and then eventual abandonment of Augusta and her children. In *The Antiphon*, however, Barnes also refers to her father's arrangement of her loss of virginity, and her feelings of bewilderment, humiliation and pain as a result of both the act of violation and her mother and grandmother's failure to prevent it. This event stands at the centre of Augusta and Miranda's relationship, although is rather obscured in the published text by Eliot's cutting of lines, in earlier drafts attributed to Dudley, in which he describes the act of rape itself. What remains is only the brothers' accusation that their mother ignored Miranda's cries for help: 'Still you swept the strings, and still she cried/ "My mother, O my mother" ' (*A* 168). If in *Ryder* Barnes had worked into fiction her ambiguous admiration and resentment of her father, and in *Nightwood* exorcized the spectre of Thelma Wood, in *The Antiphon* she turned to the memory of her mother. For in the absence of Titus and his mother, Augusta alone remains to blame, culpable for her complicity in her husband's destructive philosophy of free love. When Augusta arrives in Act II, Jeremy presents her with the doll's house, stating 'Madam, your contagion', whilst Elisha viciously cries 'Feed her to the toy!' (*A* 181). Faced with the past, Augusta collapses screaming.

In contrast to her brothers, who seek revenge in violent verbal and physical attacks, Miranda remains wearily calm and detached. Barnes herself, however, refused to spare her mother when she was writing the text, reproaching her for events for which her grandmother Zadel was probably more to blame. Her attack possibly resulted from anger at more recent insults, notably Elizabeth's coldness when her daughter was in the Lake George sanatorium. Aggrieved at what she regarded as her mother's continued abandonment of her, Barnes poured her torment into *The Antiphon*, telling Willa Muir that in writing the play she was 'as savage as a dagger', and describing herself in the role of Miranda as 'a deadly beloved vixen' (*A* 99).[10] Well aware of the family's discomfort at the revelations of *Ryder*, and as if predicting what would have been Elizabeth Barnes's response to her daughter's later and more vitriolic attack, Barnes has Augusta say to Miranda, 'May God protect us! I wonder what you'll write/ When I am dead and gone!' (*A* 209). Within the play, Augusta prevents any such possibility by bringing the great bell crashing down upon them both.

The final act with its tragic denouement takes place after dinner and involves only Miranda and Augusta, the brothers having gone to bed. Augusta regrets her naïvety as a young girl, and in old age now attempts to return to her youth again and block out the events of her adult life. 'Let us play' (*A* 193), she says, fantasizing that she is Helen of Troy, the Empress Josephine and Lillie Langtry. She criticizes her daughter's life as frivolous and immoral, but in reality envies her freedoms. 'Is it true that you had forty lovers?' (*A* 204) she asks, in a voyeuristic fascination with her daughter's sexual relationships that she disguises as chaste horror. Miranda refuses to displace the past or relieve her mother of her charge of guilt, demanding:

> Be not your own pathetic fallacy, but be
> Your own dark measure in the vein,
> For we're about a tragic business, mother.

(A 205)

Augusta, however, avoids having to admit her part in her daughter's rape by denying Titus's involvement. 'If you are speaking of your father, I forgive him' *(A* 208), she states, shouting at the end, 'You are to blame, to blame, you are to blame' *(A* 223), as she kills both her daughter and herself.

Despite Eliot's dour predictions, *The Antiphon* premièred on stage only three years after publication to wide praise in reviews. Muir had recommended the play to Dag Hammarskjlöd, secretary general for the United Nations, who in turn showed it to the respected director of the Dramaten (the Royal Dramatic Theatre of Sweden), Karl Ragnar Gierow, who had directed the première of Eugene O'Neill's *Long Day's Journey into Night*. Extremely impressed with *The Antiphon*, he and Hammarskjöld translated the play, after careful consultation with Barnes, for production in Stockholm in 1961. The first translation of *Nightwood* had been into Swedish, in 1956, and with the performance of *The Antiphon*, Barnes was accorded celebrity status, reviews describing the play as difficult and mysterious, but also powerful and fascinating. That the play should have been successful after it had been severely criticized by Eliot was perhaps not as surprising as it may seem. Despite difficulties in the interpretation of her often archaic language and complexly allusive meanings, Barnes's writings have been translated into French, German, Italian and Spanish, as well as Swedish, in some cases the translations being of work not available in English publication.[11] Moreover, Phillip Herring draws attention to the sustained but often overlooked European appreciation of Barnes's work, noting that from the 1950s she received 'more respect on the European continent than in English-speaking countries'.[12]

Barnes's later years were lived in almost total seclusion, and she was hostile to unknown visitors and interviewers. The deaths of Muir, Hammarskjöld and Eliot, close friends who had highly esteemed and promoted her work, shocked her deeply, and were combined with the losses of Dan Mahoney and, in the 1970s, Thelma Wood, Natalie Barney and Emily Coleman. 'How do writers keep on writing?', Barnes wrote in 1963, continuing, 'Professional ones do, I don't see how my kind can – the "passion spent," and even the fury – the passion made into *Nightwood* the fury (nearly) exhausted in *The Antiphon* . . . what is left? "The horror," as Conrad put it'.[13] She did keep writing, however, working on poems which she was continually revising and rewriting. Two were published in her lifetime, 'Quarry' and 'The Walking-mort', both in the *New Yorker*, and *Creatures in an Alphabet*, a bestiary, posthumously in 1982. In a letter to Emily Coleman from London in February 1939, Barnes included a long quote from *Le Temps retrouvé* in which Proust states that 'we are not at all free in the presence of the work of art to be created, that we do not do it as we ourselves please, but that it existed prior to us and we should seek to discover it as we would a natural law because it is both necessary and hidden'.[14] 'Quarry' continues this recognition of the influence of memory and a sense of prehistory that lies before it, and offers an appropriate epitaph for Barnes, describing the palimpsest of memory that she mined for all her major work, forcing the poetic soul into life, and words from the silence of the past:

> While I unwind duration from the tongue-tied tree,
> Send carbon fourteen down for time's address.
> The old revengeful without memory
> Stand by –
> I come, I come that path and there look in
> And see the capsized eye of sleep and wrath
> And hear the beaters' 'Gone to earth!'
> Then do I sowl the soul and slap its face
> That it fetch breath.

Notes

INTRODUCTION

1. Djuna Barnes, 'Vagaries Malicieux', *The Double Dealer*, May 1922, 256.
2. Djuna Barnes to Elizabeth Chappell Barnes, 19 February 1923. All letters are in the Djuna Barnes archive at the McKeldin Library, University of Maryland, unless otherwise cited.
3. Henry Raymont, 'From the Avant-Garde of the Thirties, Djuna Barnes', *New York Times*, 24 May 1971, 24.
4. Edwin Muir, *The Present Age from 1914* (London: Cresset Press, 1939), 150.
5. Peter Nicholls, *Modernisms: A Literary Guide* (Basingstoke: Macmillan, 1995), 222.
6. Emily Coleman to Djuna Barnes, 27 August 1935.

CHAPTER 1. FLEUR DU MAL: EARLY WRITINGS

1. Guido Bruno, 'Fleurs du mal à la mode de New York', *Pearson's Magazine* (1919), reprinted in Djuna Barnes, *Interviews*, edited by Alyce Barry (Los Angeles: Sun & Moon Press, 1985), 388.
2. See Michael C. Emery, *The Press and America: An Interpretative History of the Mass Media* (Englewood Cliffs, NJ: Prentice-Hall, 1988).
3. Lydia Steptoe, 'Against Nature: In Which Everything that is Young, Inadequate and Tiresome is Included in the Term Natural', *Vanity Fair*, August 1922, 60, 78.
4. Lydia Steptoe, 'What is Good Form in Dying? In Which a Dozen Dainty Deaths Are Suggested for Daring Damsels', *Vanity Fair*, June 1923, 73, 102.
5. See, for example, Nancy J. Levine, ' "Bringing Milkshakes to Bulldogs": The Early Journalism of Djuna Barnes', in Mary Lynn

Broe (ed.), *Silence and Power: A Reevaluation of Djuna Barnes* (Carbondale: Southern Illinois University Press, 1991), and Carolyn Allen, 'Writing toward *Nightwood*: Djuna Barnes' Seduction Stories', in Broe, *Silence and Power*, 54–65.

6. Djuna Barnes, 'The Hem of Manhattan', *New York Morning Telegraph Sunday Magazine*, 29 July 1917, 2; reprinted in Djuna Barnes, *New York*, edited by Alyce Barry (Los Angeles: Sun & Moon Press, 1987), 290.

7. Djuna Barnes, 'Surcease in Hurry and Whirl – On the Restless Surf at Coney', *New York Morning Telegraph Sunday Magazine*, 15 July 1917, 2; in Barry (ed.), *New York*, 275–84.

8. Djuna Barnes, 'My Adventures Being Rescued', *New York World Magazine*, 14 November 1915; in Barry (ed.) *New York*, 185–9, 187.

9. Ibid., 189.

10. Djuna Barnes, 'How It Feels to be Forcibly Fed', *New York World Magazine*, 6 September 1914; in Barry (ed.), *New York*, 174–9.

11. Ibid., 178.

12. Djuna Barnes, 'Greenwich Village As It Is', *Pearson's Magazine*, October 1916; in Barry (ed.), *New York*, 230, 227, 226.

13. Djuna Barnes, 'Becoming Intimate with the Bohemians', *New York Morning Telegraph Sunday Magazine*, 19 November 1916; in Barry (ed.), *New York*, 242.

14. 'How the Villagers Amuse Themselves', *New York Morning Telegraph Sunday Magazine*, 26 November 1916; in Barry (ed.), *New York*, 246.

15. Phillip Herring, *Djuna: The Life and Works of Djuna Barnes* (New York: Viking, 1995), 88.

16. 'And Yet Again; The Bayes Still Scene of One-Act Plays', *New York Sunday Telegraph*, 7 May 1926, 26.

17. *New York Evening Post*, 7 May 1926, 14.

18. Lawrence Langner, *The Magic Curtain* (New York: E. P. Dutton, 1951), 110.

19. 'Aller et Retour', *transatlantic review*, 1 (April 1924); 'Cassation', originally 'A Little Girl Tells a Story to a Lady', in *Contact Collection of Contemporary Writers* (Paris: Three Mountains Press, 1925); 'The Grande Malade', originally 'The Little Girl Continues', in *This Quarter*, 1 (Fall 1925); 'Dusie', in *American Esoterica* (New York: Macy-Masius, 1927). 'Behind the Heart' was written for Charles Henri Ford during their affair in 1931–2. It remained unpublished until discovered in the Ford papers at the Harry Ransom Humanities Research Centre, University of Texas-Austin by Mary Lynn Broe, modernist scholar and Ford's literary executor. All these stories are now available in their revised forms

in Djuna Barnes, *Collected Stories*, ed. Phillip Herring (Los Angeles: Sun & Moon Classics, 1997). Textual references refer to Herring's edition.

20. Djuna Barnes, 'The Models Have Come to Town', *Charm*, November 1924. See also Mary Lynn Broe, ' "A love from the back of the heart": The Story Djuna Wrote for Charles Henri', in *Review of Contemporary Fiction* (1993), 22–32.
21. Carolyn Allen, 'Writing toward *Nightwood*: Djuna Barnes' Seduction Stories', in Broe, *Silence and Power*, 54–65.
22. See Herring, *Djuna*.

CHAPTER 2. A FEMALE COMIC EPIC: *RYDER*

1. Quoted in Andrew Field, *Djuna: The Life and Times of Djuna Barnes* (New York: Putnam's, 1983), 127.
2. Djuna Barnes, 'James Joyce', *Vanity Fair*, April 1922, 104.
3. The illustrations, one depicting 'Beast Thingumbob' and another a soprano urinating in the street, are reprinted in the 1990 edition of *Ryder* published by the Dalkey Archive Press.
4. C. Hartley Grattan, 'A Lusty Book', *New York Evening Sun*, 1 August 1928.
5. Review of *Ryder* (St Martin's Press, 1980), *San Francisco Review of Books*, 7 April 1980, 6.
6. Herring, *Djuna*, 43.
7. Margot Norris, *Beasts of the Modern Imagination* (Baltimore: Johns Hopkins University Press, 1985), 3.
8. Ibid.
9. Review of *Ryder*, *San Francisco Review of Books*, March 1980 (Djuna Barnes archive, McKeldin Library, University of Maryland).

CHAPTER 3. SAPPHIC SATIRE: *LADIES ALMANACK*

1. Quoted in Karen Lane Rood (ed.), *American Writers in Paris, 1920–1939* (Detroit: Gale, 1980), 44.
2. Louis F. Kannenstine, *The Art of Djuna Barnes: Duality and Damnation* (New York: New York University Press, 1977), 47; Karla Jay, 'The Outsider among the Expatriates: Djuna Barnes' Satire on the Ladies of the *Almanack*', in Broe, *Silence and Power*, 184–93.
3. Quoted in Shari Benstock, *Women of the Left Bank: Paris 1900–1940* (London: Virago, 1987), 264.
4. Shari Benstock, 'Paris Lesbianism and the Politics of Reaction, 1900–1940', in Martin Bauml Duberman, Martha Vicinus and

George Chauncey Jr (eds.), *Hidden from History: Reclaiming the Gay and Lesbian Past* (London: Penguin, 1991), 343.

5. Janet Flanner, *Paris Was Yesterday: 1925–1939* (New York: The Viking Press, 1972), p. xvii.
6. Elyse Blankley, 'Return to Mytilène: Renée Vivien and the City of Women', in Susan Merrill Squier (ed.), *Women Writers and the City* (Knoxville: University of Tennessee Press, 1984), 49.
7. Benstock, *Women of the Left Bank*, 249.
8. Jeffrey Weeks, *Sex, Politics and Society: The Regulation of Sexuality Since 1800* (London: Longman, 1981), 115.
9. See, for example, Bridget Elliott and Jo-Ann Wallace, *Women Artists and Writers: Modernist (im)positionings* (London: Routledge, 1994).
10. Flanner, *Paris Was Yesterday*, 48.

CHAPTER 4. BARNES'S HILARIOUS SORROW: *NIGHTWOOD*

1. Djuna Barnes to Emily Coleman, 23 June 1935, quoted in Cheryl Plumb, *Fancy's Craft: Art and Identity in the Early Works of Djuna Barnes* (Pennsylvania: Susquehanna, 1986), p. viii.
2. Philip Rahv, 'The Taste of Nothing, *The New Masses*', quoted in Jane Marcus, 'Mousemeat: Contemporary Reviews of *Nightwood*', in Broe, *Silence and Power*, 200.
3. C. L. Watson, 'Mr Eliot Presents Miss Barnes', *Brooklyn Eagle*, 7 March 1937; Review of *Nightwood, New Statesman and Nation*, 17 October 1936; Rose C. Feld, 'Ruthless Tragic Laughter', *New York Herald Tribune*, 3 July 1937. (Djuna Barnes archive, McKeldin Library, University of Maryland.)
4. Dylan Thomas, 'Night Wood', *Oxford and Cambridge Journal*, March 1937, 27.
5. Jane Marcus, 'Laughing at Leviticus: Nightwood as Woman's Circus Epic', in Broe, *Silence and Power*, 223.
6. Barnes and Ford visited Vienna, Budapest and Munich, and were introduced to the German philosopher Oswald Spengler, author of the widely influential *The Decline of the West* (1918–22), by Barnes's ex-lover Putzi Hafstaengl. Hafstaengl also tried to arrange an interview for Barnes with Adolf Hitler, but it never took place, due to the exorbitant fee Hitler requested.
7. The importance of medical, social-scientific and psychological theory for modernist literary experimentation is explored by Tim Armstrong, *Modernism, Technology and the Body: A Cultural Study* (Cambridge: Cambridge University Press, 1998).

8. Michel Foucault, *The History of Sexuality*, vol. 1, *An Introduction*, trans. Robert Hurley (New York: Vintage, 1980).
9. Ibid., 43.
10. Jane Marcus, 'Laughing at Leviticus', 233.
11. Radclyffe Hall, *The Well of Loneliness* (London: Virago, 1982), 207.
12. Richard von Krafft-Ebing, *Psychopathia Sexualis, with Especial Reference to the Antipathic Sexual Instinct*, trans. Franklin S. Klaf (London: Staples Press, 1965), 188.
13. Ann Douglas, *Terrible Honesty: Mongrel Manhattan in the 1920s* (London: Picador, 1996), 124.
14. Public transvestitism had been made a punishable offence, except during Carnival, in 1853. See Vernon A. Rosario, *The Erotic Imagination: French Histories of Perversity* (Oxford: Oxford University Press, 1997).
15. Jay Prosser, 'Transsexuals and the Transsexologists: Inversion and the Emergence of Transsexual Subjectivity', in Lucy Bland and Laura Doan (eds.), *Sexology in Culture: Labelling Bodies and Desires* (Cambridge: Polity, 1998), 122. The 1920s German debate on homosexuality was polarized between the masculine–feminine definition advocated by Hirschfeld and the ultra-masculine definition of Hans Blüher. See James D. Steakley, *The Homosexual Emancipation Movement in Germany* (New York: Arno Press, 1975).
16. Robert McAlmon and Kay Boyle, *Being Geniuses Together, 1920–1930* (London: Hogarth Press, 1984), 96, 98.
17. Ibid., 95.
18. Ibid., 96.
19. Jeffrey Weeks, 'Havelock Ellis and the Politics of Sex Reform', in Sheila Rowbotham and Jeffrey Weeks, *Socialism and the New Life: The Personal and Sexual Politics of Edward Carpenter and Havelock Ellis* (London: Pluto Press, 1977), 155.
20. Bonnie Kime Scott, *Rethinking Modernism*, vol. 2, *Postmodern Feminist Readings of Woolf, West and Barnes* (Bloomington: Indiana University Press, 1995), 72. Kime Scott goes on to argue, for example, that the notorious final scene of 'Bow Down' is 'suggestive of ritual healing, arguing that both beast and human have a therapeutic run through the emotions, full of gesture, movement, and even pain' (p. 117).
21. Diane Chisholm, 'Obscene Modernism: *Eros Noir* and the Profane Illumination of Djuna Barnes', *American Literature*, 69:1 (1997), 167–205, 176.
22. Joseph Allen Boone, *Libidinal Currents: Sexuality and the Shaping of Modernism* (Chicago: University of Chicago Press, 1998).
23. Ibid., 234, 7.

24. Michel de Certeau, *The Practice of Everyday Life* (Berkeley: University of California Press, 1988), 94. *Espace propre* translates as 'clean' and 'proper', as well as 'own space'.
25. Letters in the Barnes archive at the University of Maryland suggest that he may have performed the abortion that Barnes underwent in 1930 or 1931.
26. John Glassco, *Memoirs of Montparnasse* (Oxford: Oxford University Press, 1995), 20.
27. Herring, *Djuna*, 210; Charles Henri Ford, quoted in Herring, *Djuna*, 212.
28. Djuna Barnes to Daniel Mahoney, 14 November, 1958.
29. Stanley Edgar Hyman, Review of *Selected Works, New Leader*, 16 April 1962.
30. Djuna Barnes to Emily Coleman, 20 September 1935, Emily Holms Coleman Papers, Special Collections, University of Delaware, Newark, Delaware.
31. T. R. Smith to Djuna Barnes, 29 August 1934.
32. T. S. Eliot to Geoffrey Faber, quoted in Herring, *Djuna*, 231.
33. Marcus, 'Laughing at Leviticus', 237; Herring, *Djuna*, 233; Tyrus Miller, *Late Modernism: Politics, Fiction and the Arts Between the World Wars* (Berkeley: University of California Press, 1999), 122.
34. Djuna Barnes, *Nightwood: The Original Version and Related Drafts* (Illinois: Dalkey Archive Press, 1995), 262.
35. *New York Times Book Review*, 17 July 1983, 23.
36. Chisholm, 'Obscene Modernism', 188, my italics.
37. Quoted in Vern L. Bullough and Bonnie Bullough, *Sin, Sickness, and Sanity: A History of Sexual Attitudes* (New York: Garland, 1977), 170.
38. Maud Ellmann, *The Poetics of Impersonality: Eliot and Pound* (Brighton: Harvester, 1987), 93.
39. Miller, *Late Modernism*, 147.

CHAPTER 5. EPILOGUE: *THE ANTIPHON*

1. Quoted by Burke, in Broe, *Silence and Power*, 72.
2. *Town and Country*, December 1941.
3. Djuna Barnes to Emily Coleman, 11 December 1937 (Djuna Barnes archive, McKeldin Libary, University of Maryland).
4. See Lynda Curry, ' "Tom, Take Mercy": Djuna Barnes' Drafts of *The Antiphon*', in Broe, *Silence and Power*, 286–98, for an analysis of these cuts in relation to earlier drafts of the play.
5. Sheet in the Barnes archive at the McKeldin Library, on which Barnes has written 'Blurb by T. S. Eliot!'

6. Djuna Barnes to T. S. Eliot, 9 January 1957.
7. T. S. Eliot to Djuna Barnes, 4 June 1957.
8. Djuna Barnes to Emily Coleman, 25 March 1940.
9. Djuna Barnes to Emily Coleman, 30 March 1940.
10. Djuna Barnes to Willa Muir, 23 July 1961.
11. See Douglas Messerli, *Djuna Barnes: A Bibliography* (New York: David Lewis, 1975). Of European publishers, Wagenbach in Berlin and IGITUR in Barcelona have published translations of extensive sections of Barnes's work.
12. Herring, *Djuna*, 278.
13. Djuna Barnes to Peter Hoare, 18 July 1963, quoted in Broe, *Silence and Power*, 337.
14. Djuna Barnes to Emily Coleman, 4 February 1939.

Select Bibliography

BIBLIOGRAPHY

Messerli, Douglas, *Djuna Barnes: A Bibliography* (New York: David Lewis, 1975). A definitive bibliography of Barnes's writing.

WORKS BY DJUNA BARNES

The Book of Repulsive Women: Eight Rhythms and Five Drawings (New York: Bruno's Chapbooks II, no. 6, 1915; Los Angeles: Sun & Moon Press, 1989).

A Book (New York: Boni & Liveright, 1923).

Ryder (New York: Boni & Liveright, 1928; Illinois: Dalkey Archive, 1990).

Ladies Almanack (Dijon, France: Darantière, 1928; New York: Harper & Row, 1972; Illinois: Dalkey Archive, 1992).

A Night Among the Horses (New York: Boni & Liveright, 1929).

Nightwood (London: Faber & Faber, 1936, 1950; New York: Harcourt Brace, 1937).

The Antiphon (London: Faber & Faber, 1958; New York: Farrar, Straus, 1958).

The Selected Works of Djuna Barnes (Spillway, The Antiphon, Nightwood), (New York: Farrar, Straus and Cudahy, 1962; London: Faber & Faber, 1980).

Creatures in an Alphabet (New York: Dial Press, 1982).

Smoke and Other Early Stories, edited by Douglas Messerli (Los Angeles: Sun & Moon Press, 1982).

Interviews, edited by Alyce Barry (Los Angeles: Sun & Moon Press, 1985).

New York, edited by Alyce Barry (Los Angeles: Sun & Moon Press, 1987).

Poe's Mother, edited by Douglas Messerli (Los Angeles: Sun & Moon Press, 1995).

At the Roots of the Stars: The Short Plays, edited by Douglas Messerli (Los Angeles: Sun & Moon Press, 1995).

Nightwood: The Original Version and Related Drafts, edited by Cheryl J. Plumb (Illinois: Dalkey Archive, 1995).

The Collected Stories of Djuna Barnes, edited by Phillip Herring (Los Angeles: Sun & Moon Press, 1997).

BIOGRAPHICAL AND CRITICAL STUDIES

Collections of Essays

Broe, Mary Lynn (ed.), *Silence and Power: A Reevaluation of Djuna Barnes* (Carbondale: Southern Illinois University Press, 1991). An essential collection on Barnes, including scholarly essays, extracts from letters and reviews, photographs and recollections by friends and interviewers.

Levine, Nancy J., and Marian Urquilla (eds.), *Djuna Barnes, Review of Contemporary Fiction Special Issue*, 13:3 (1993). An excellent collection of essays from a range of scholarly perspectives, with particular emphasis on feminist criticism.

Individual Books and Essays

Allen, Carolyn, *Following Djuna: Women Lovers and the Erotics of Loss* (Bloomington, IN: Indiana University Press, 1996). A useful discussion of Barnes in relation to other women writers, highlighting issues of gender and lesbianism.

Benstock, Shari, *Women of the Left Bank: Paris, 1900–1940* (London: Virago, 1987). A fascinating and comprehensive account of the lives and work of women expatriate writers, patrons and publishers in Paris, focusing on their response to and representation of the city.

Boone, Joseph Allen, *Libidinal Currents: Sexuality and the Shaping of Modernism* (Chicago: University of Chicago Press, 1992). An excellent study that focuses on an urban modernist imagination of the marginal, and cites *Nightwood* amongst a number of texts that engage with psychosexual forces that challenge conventional readings of modernism.

Broe, Mary Lynn, 'My Art Belongs to Daddy: Incest as Exile – The Textual Economics of Hayford Hall', in Mary Lynn Broe and Angela Ingram (eds.), *Women's Writing in Exile* (Chapel Hill, NC: University of North Carolina Press, 1989), 41–86. Discusses Barnes's periods of writing at Peggy Guggenheim's English mansion Hayford Hall.

Carlston, Erin, *Thinking Fascism: Sapphic Modernism and Fascist Modernity* (Stanford: Stanford University Press, 1998). Analyses *Nightwood* as part of a provocative study on the engagement of a 'Sapphic Modernism' with fascist politics and ideology.

Chisholm, Diane, 'Obscene Modernism: *Eros Noir* and the Profane Illumination of Djuna Barnes', *American Literature*, 69:1 (1997), 167–205. An insightful and compelling essay that analyses *Nightwood* in relation to Walter Benjamin's theory of 'profane illumination'.

Curry, Lynda, ' "Tom, Take Mercy" ': Djuna Barnes's Drafts of *The Antiphon'*, in Mary Lynn Broe (ed.), *Silence and Power: A Reevaluation of Djuna Barnes* (Carbondale: Southern Illinois University Press, 1991), 286–98. An important and invaluable essay on T. S. Eliot's cuts to *The Antiphon*.

DeVore, Lynn, 'The Backgrounds of *Nightwood*: Robin, Felix, and Nora', *Journal of Modern Literature*, 10 (March 1983), 71–90. An interesting and well-researched account of possible sources and influences for the characters in *Nightwood*.

Elliott, Bridget, and Jo-Ann Wallace, *Women Artists and Writers: Modernist (im)positionings* (London: Routledge, 1994). Includes an excellent discussion of Barnes's early writings in relation to the influence of Decadence.

Field, Andrew, *Djuna: The Life and Times of Djuna Barnes* (Austin, TX: University of Texas Press, 1985). An interesting biographical study, although poorly documented and less accurate than that of Herring (see below).

Frank, Joseph, 'Djuna Barnes: *Nightwood'*, in *The Widening Gyre: Crisis and Mastery in Modern Literature* (New Brunswick: Rutgers University Press, 1963), 25–49. An important early essay that discusses *Nightwood* in terms of 'spatial form' as an exemplar of the canonical modernist text.

Fuchs, Miriam, 'Djuna Barnes and T. S. Eliot: Authority, Resistance and Acquiescence', *Tulsa Studies in Women's Literature*, 12:2 (1993), 289–313. An excellent discussion of Barnes's relationship with T. S. Eliot.

Galvin, Mary E., *Queer Poetics: Five Modernist Women Writers* (Westport, CT: Greenwood Press, 1999). An illuminating analysis of *The Book of Repulsive Women* from the perspective of queer theory.

Herring, Phillip, *Djuna: The Life and Work of Djuna Barnes* (New York: Viking, 1995). The best recent biography, extensively researched and documented.

Kaivola, Karen, *All Contraries Confounded: The Lyrical Fiction of Virginia Woolf, Djuna Barnes, and Marguerite Duras* (Iowa: University of Iowa Press, 1991). An insightful analysis of the contradictory impulses and ambivalences in *Nightwood* as Barnes attempts to challenge cultural norms.

Kannenstine, Louis F., *The Art of Djuna Barnes: Duality and Damnation* (New York: New York University Press, 1977). One of the early critical studies of Barnes, highlighting the frequent representation of dualities such as animal vs. human and nature vs. civilization in her work.

Kime Scott, Bonnie, *Refiguring Modernism*, vol. 2, *Postmodern Feminist Readings of Woolf, West and Barnes* (Bloomington, IN: Indiana University Press, 1995). An excellent critical study of strategies by which Barnes challenges the narratives of male modernist texts, with a particular focus on the breakdown of binary divisions in her work.

Marcus, Jane, 'Laughing at Leviticus: *Nightwood* as Woman's Circus Epic', in Mary Lynn Broe (ed.), *Silence and Power: A Reevaluation of Djuna Barnes* (Carbondale: Southern Illinois University Press, 1991), 221–50. An excellent and ground-breaking study that argues for recognition of Barnes's 'political unconscious', focusing on the transgression of social order in *Nightwood* through the violation of the taboo.

—— 'Mousemeat: Contemporary Reviews of *Nightwood*', in Mary Lynn Broe (ed.), *Silence and Power: A Reevaluation of Djuna Barnes* (Carbondale: Southern Illinois University Press, 1991), 195–204. A useful collection of reviews from the Barnes archive at the University of Maryland.

Miller, Tyrus, *Late Modernism: Politics, Fiction, and the Arts Between the World Wars* (Berkeley: University of California Press, 1999). An illuminating study of Barnes and modernism in the context of the social and politically turbulent years of the late 1920s and 1930s.

Scott, James B., *Djuna Barnes* (Boston: Twayne Publishers, 1976). A useful early account that discusses all of Barnes's major work.

BACKGROUND READING

Anderson, Margaret, *My Thirty Years War* (New York: Horizon, 1970).

Armstrong, Tim, *Modernism, Technology and the Body: A Cultural Study* (Cambridge: Cambridge University Press, 1998).

Barney, Natalie Clifford, *Adventures of the Mind* (New York: New York University Press, 1992).

Bauml Duberman, Martin, Martha Vicinus and George Chauncey Jr (eds.), *Hidden from History: Reclaiming the Gay and Lesbian Past* (London: Penguin, 1991).

Bland, Lucy, and Laura Doan (eds.), *Sexology in Culture: Labelling Bodies and Desires* (Cambridge: Polity, 1998).

Butler, Judith, *Gender Trouble: Feminism and the Subversion of Identity* (New York: Routledge, 1990).

Douglas, Ann, *Terrible Honesty: Mongrel Manhattan in the 1920s* (London: Picador, 1996).

Ellmann, Maud, *The Poetics of Impersonality: Eliot and Pound* (Brighton: Harvester, 1987).

Emery, Michael C., *The Press and America: An Interpretative History of the Mass Media* (Englewood Cliffs, NJ: Prentice-Hall, 1988).

Flanner, Janet, *Paris Was Yesterday: 1925–1939* (New York: The Viking Press, 1972).

Foucault, Michel, *The History of Sexuality*, vol. 1, *An Introduction*, trans. Robert Hurley (New York: Vintage, 1980).

Friedman, Ellen G., and Miriam Fuchs, *Breaking the Sequence: Women's Experimental Fiction* (Princeton: Princeton University Press, 1989).

Glassco, John, *Memoirs of Montparnasse* (New York: Viking, 1973).

Hall, Radclyffe, *The Well of Loneliness* (London: Virago, 1982).

Hanscombe, Gillian E., and Virginia L. Smyers, *Writing for Their Lives: Modernist Women, 1910–1940* (London: The Women's Press, 1987).

Heron, Liz, *Streets of Desire: Women's Fictions of the Twentieth-Century City* (London: Virago, 1993).

Krafft-Ebing, Richard von, *Psychopathia Sexualis, with Especial Reference to the Antipathic Sexual Instinct*, trans. Franklin S. Klaf (London: Staples Press, 1965).

Langner, Lawrence, *The Magic Curtain* (New York: E. P. Dutton, 1951).

McAlmon, Robert, and Kay Boyle, *Being Geniuses Together, 1920–1930* (London: Hogarth Press, 1984).

Muir, Edwin, *The Present Age from 1914* (London: Cresset Press, 1939).

Nicholls, Peter, *Modernisms: A Literary Guide* (Basingstoke: Macmillan, 1995).

Norris, Margot, *Beasts of the Modern Imagination* (Baltimore, MD: Johns Hopkins University Press, 1985).

Rood, Karen Lane (ed.), *American Writers in Paris, 1920–1939* (Detroit: Gale, 1980).

Rosario, Vernon A., *The Erotic Imagination: French Histories of Perversity* (Oxford: Oxford University Press, 1997).

Sedgwick, Eve Kosofsky, *Novel Gazing: Queer Reading in Fiction* (Durham, NC: Duke University Press, 1997).

Squier, Susan Merrill (ed.), *Women Writers and the City* (Knoxville: University of Tennessee Press, 1984).

Steakley, James D., *The Homosexual Emancipation Movement in Germany* (New York: Arno Press, 1975).

Weeks, Jeffrey, *Sex, Politics and Society: The Regulation of Sexuality Since 1800* (London: Longman, 1981).

Index